Lecture Notes in Computer Science 7545

Commenced Publication in 1973
Founding and Former Series Editors:
Gerhard Goos, Juris Hartmanis, and Jan van Leeuwen

Francisco Cipolla-Ficarra   Kim Veltman
Miguel Cipolla-Ficarra   Andreas Kratky (Eds.)

Communicability, Computer Graphics and Innovative Design for Interactive Systems

First International Symposium, CCGIDIS 2011
Córdoba, Spain, June 28-29, 2011
Revised Selected Papers

 Springer

Volume Editors

Francisco Cipolla-Ficarra
Miguel Cipolla-Ficarra
ALAIPO and AINCI, HCI Lab.
Via Tabajani 1 - Suc. 15 (CP 7), 24121 Bergamo, Italy
E-mail: ficarra@alaipo.com, ficarra@ainci.com

Kim Veltman
Virtual Maastricht McLuhan Institute
Europalaan 73, 6226 CN, Maastricht, The Netherlands
E-mail: kim_veltman@hotmail.com

Andreas Kratky
University of Southern California
Interactive Media Division, School of Cinematic Arts
900 West 34th Street, SCA 201, Los Angeles, CA 90089-2211, USA
E-mail: akratky@cinema.usc.edu

ISSN 0302-9743   e-ISSN 1611-3349
ISBN 978-3-642-33759-8   e-ISBN 978-3-642-33760-4
DOI 10.1007/978-3-642-33760-4
Springer Heidelberg Dordrecht London New York

Library of Congress Control Number: 2012949334

CR Subject Classification (1998): H.5.1-3, H.4.3, I.3.7-8, C.5.3, H.5.5

LNCS Sublibrary: SL 3 – Information Systems and Application, incl. Internet/Web
and HCI

Typesetting: Camera-ready by author, data conversion by Scientific Publishing Services, Chennai, India

Printed on acid-free paper

Springer is part of Springer Science+Business Media (www.springer.com)

Preface

Since ancient times, units of measure have been a historic landmark in the evolution of humankind. Computers have quickly introduced, from scientific language to colloquial language, the minimal unit of information, such as the bit, in the first stage of its evolution. Before the end of the twentieth century, the pixel was another term that was vigorously introduced into the daily vocabulary of millions of people on all the continents of our planet. Today the worth that the pixel has, now that it has been democratized, is incalculable. If we add to this the possibility of emulating and simulating reality, in 2D and/or 3D, its borders are expanding as time goes on.

The secret of the correct expansion, with limited costs for the population, professionals, researchers, etc., will depend to a great extent on the surrender of the power exerted from certain environments in the formal sciences for several decades. In this regard it is easy to establish organization charts that make up the map of those who held the power in the graphical software and hardware sector during the last two decades of the twentieth century, such as has been the case in industrial engineering in Spain, audiovisual technology in France, physicists, electrical engineers and computer experts in Italy, etc. Experts capable of solving the hardware issues and who little by little introduced to the software environment. The before and the after, whether it is in the concentration of knowledge, as in its distribution, took place with the cheapening of computers and peripherals of graphical computing and the appearance of a commercial software for graphic design with a high quality and of universal distribution.

Graphic design applied to industry sped up the production processes and made them easier. Humans with their creative power and personal computers allowed one to open new R+D environments. Currently, thanks to innovative design, many industries can widen their products' export and/or services to the rest of the world. Not for nothing the "made in" label is starting to be replaced by "style." The original style is the synthesis of that innovative design which makes a product and/or service be unique among its peers. Evidently, this is thanks to telecommunications and the new technologies related to computer science. Inside a successful design, communicability is always to be found.

The varied applications of the display screen prove this statement in areas such as 3D TV (immersive and frameless design), the wall-format (touch sensitive and seamless design), the work surface (versatile and application enabling), and the flexible display (ultrathin and rollable). Without forgetting the organic user interfaces, the brain computer interfaces (the interaction times user-computer will be milliseconds), among so many other discoveries and inventions that take place every day in the ICT environment. Our modest and main objective is to examine the latest breakthroughs and the future trends, within the communicability, computer graphics, and innovative design of interactive systems triad, for the well-being of humanity.

The papers in this volume were presented at the Program Committee of the symposium consisted of Albert, C. (Spain), Anderson, S. (USA), Bleecker, J. (USA), Buzzi, M. (Italy), Cáceres-Díaz, A. (Puerto Rico), Carré, J. (Curaçao), Casas, S. (Argentina), Chorianopoulos, K. (Greece), Cipolla-Ficarra, M. (Italy & Spain), Colorado, A. (Spain), Brie, M. (Malta), Dalmasso, M. (Argentina), Darmawan, R. (Indonesia), de Castro-Lozano, C. (Spain), Demirors, O. (Turkey), Díaz-Pérez, P. (Spain), Edison, D. (Canada), El Sadik, A. (Canada), Fekonja Peklaj, U. (Slovenia), Fotouhi, F. (USA), Flores, S. (Spain), Fulton, P. (Canada), Garrido-Lora, M. (Spain), Griffith, S. (Jamaica), Grosky, W. (USA), Guarinos-Galán, V. (Spain), Guerrero-Ginel, J. (Spain), Hadad, G. (Argentina), Ilavarasan, V. (India), Imaz, M. (United Kingdom), Jen, W. (Taiwan), Kratky, A. (USA), Lau, A. (Australia), Lau, F. (China), Levialdi-Ghiron, S. (Italy), Liudmila, P. (Russia), Marcos, C. (Argentina), Milrad, M. (Sweden), Moreno-Sánchez, I. (Spain), Mori, G. (Italy), Možina, K. (Slovenia), Ramirez-Alvarado, M. (Spain), Read, T. (Spain), Sainz-de Abajo, B. (Spain), Salvendy, G. (China), Silva-Salmerón, J. (Canada), Stanchev, P. (USA), Styliaras, G. (Greece), Tamai, T. (Japan), Varela, L. (France), Veltman, K. (The Netherlands), Vidal, G. (Argentina), Vilches-López, I. (Spain), who supported the preparation of the symposium. I would like to thank all of the authors and speakers for their effort as well as the referees for their kind collaboration. Finally, a special thanks goes to Alfred Hofmann (Springer), Anna Kramer (Springer), Christine Reiss (Springer), the University of Córdoba, EATCO Research Group, Consorcio de Turismo, Maria Ficarra (ALAIPO & AINCI), various individuals and authorities, and to all those who financially supported the international symposium.

June 2011   Francisco V. Cipolla-Ficarra

Acknowledgments

Table of Contents

Communicability, Computer Graphics and Innovative Design for
Interactive Systems 1
    Francisco V. Cipolla Ficarra

Melody Generation Based on Thematic Development Method Using
Pitch Class Set and Rhythm Complexity 14
    Chih-Fang Huang and Shu-Fang Ko

Prolepsis in Computer Animation for Children 28
    Francisco V. Cipolla Ficarra, Jacqueline Alma, and
    Miguel Cipolla-Ficarra

A Security Model for Functional Active Objects 42
    Florian Kammueller

Ergonomy, Industrial Design and Divine Proportion 51
    Francisco V. Cipolla Ficarra

Emotion-Based Rhythmic Complexity Analysis for Automated Music
Generation 67
    Chih-Fang Huang and Chi-Fang Chu

Computer Graphics for Students of the Factual Sciences 79
    Francisco V. Cipolla Ficarra, Valeria M. Ficarra, and
    Andreas Kratky

Extension of Personas Technique for the Requirements Stage 94
    John W. Castro and Silvia T. Acuña

User Attention in Nonlinear Narratives: A Case of Study 104
    Victor Socas-Guerra and Carina S. González-González

Cloud Technology: The Driving Force of Change in the Business
Environment 112
    Beatriz Sainz de Abajo, Javier Sánchez González,
    Francisco Javier Burón Fernández, Enrique García Salcines,
    Miguel López Coronado, and Carlos de Castro Lozano

Ubiquitous TV with HTML5 122
    Francisco Javier Burón Fernández, Rafael Mena,
    Beatriz Sainz de Abajo, Enrique García Salcines, and
    Carlos de Castro Lozano

Ubiquitous Cordoba, a Cultural and Ambient Assisted Living U-City
Approach 127

*José Miguel Ramírez Uceda, Remedios María Robles González,
Enrique García Salcines, Francisco Javier Burón Fernández,
Beatriz Sainz de Abajo, and Carlos de Castro Lozano*

Modeling Parallel Applications on Mobile Devices 136

*Daniel Giulianelli, Claudia Pons, Carina González, Pablo Vera,
Rocío Rodríguez, and Víctor Fernández*

Author Index 145

Communicability, Computer Graphics
and Innovative Design for Interactive Systems

Francisco V. Cipolla Ficarra[1,2]

HCI Lab. – F&F Multimedia Communications Corp.,
[1] ALAIPO: Asociación Latina de Interacción Persona-Ordenador,
[2] AINCI: Asociación Internacional de la Comunicación Interactiva,
c/ Angel Baixeras, 5 – AP 1638, 08080 Barcelona, Spain
Via Pascoli, S. 15 – CP 7, 24121 Bergamo, Italy
ficarra@alaipo.com

Abstract. We present an essential triad in the era of communicability expansion that is: graphical computing, interactive design and communicability. The notions are presented in a synchronic and diachronic way from a temporal point of view and in relation to the evolution of the technology (software and hardware), the industrial design and the interactive systems. Besides, this is about carrying out corrections with regard to the communicability notion applied to the design of interactive systems aimed at mobile multimedia and microcomputing.

Keywords: Communicability, Computer Graphics, Design, Interactive Systems, Software, Hardware, Education.

1   Introduction

In the history of computer science, the hardware was always ahead of the software. The advance of graphical peripherals has played an important role [1] [2]. This is the reason why industrial engineers occupied the centre of the landscape of graphic computing during the second half of the 20th century. In this sense they were experts in peripherals wired to the CPU (Control Processing Unit). They were devoted to breaking down each one of the components of the CTR (Cathode Ray Tube) screens and the LCD (Liquid Cristal Display) from a physical, chemical and functional point of view. In the case of the main explanation of the technique of liquid crystals, in 1980, it began with the description of the molecules of the liquids, which are distributed in a random way in all the liquids, but the direction of its main axis stays parallel to a common direction known as the director. It is a quality that was used in the models of the 80s., in which a pneumatic liquid is placed between two glass walls that aim the closest molecules, in perpendicular directions, through two octagonal microscopic scratches [1] [3]. Consequently, between the two glasses a helical rotation of the 90° molecules takes place (twisted nematic). Additionally, since both glasses act at the same time as crossed polarizer and analyzer in a rest position the

F.V. Cipolla-Ficarra et al. (Eds.): CCGIDIS 2011, LNCS 7545, pp. 1–13, 2012.
© Springer-Verlag Berlin Heidelberg 2012

helical structure makes a twist through 90° from the polarization direction and the cell becomes transparent when the light goes through it. In contrast, when a certain tension is applied to one of the plates, the helical structure is destroyed and the glass is opaque. In few words, the crystal liquids are flat and require very little energy as compared to the CRT screens, although they have a limited vision field. In this small explanation one can understand the reason of the presence of the industrial engineers in the graphic computing sector in the last century. Obviously, nowadays all these data and information can be obtained on-line by a graphic computing student and with multimedia resources, such as the animated simulations.

The genesis of the use of graphic screens cwas established in the Massachusetts Institute of Technology in 1950, wired to the computer Whirlwind 1 [4] [5]. These screens were wired to the plotters who confined themselves to depicting graphically certain equation results for a better interpretation and decision making. Now for the interaction with the computer graphics it was necessary to wait for the doctoral thesis of Ivan E. Sutherland (1962-1963), Sketchpad: A Man-Machine Graphical Communications System [4].

In fact, it was the first drawing computer program that allowed the users to draw points, line segments and circular rings directly on the screen. From then on he introduced several concepts such as the three-dimensional modelling of the computer, visual simulations, automated design, virtual reality, etc. The result of the graphic computing is the synthesis of images. In its origins the static image prevailed on the dynamic one. The interaction was very reduced, and the first images were of a vector type applied to engineering, architecture, etc. The raster screens were the first that introduced colour. In them the electron beam moves systematically sweeping the screen with a set of horizontal lines in an identical way to television technology. In these screens one can talk of a pixel matrix, which can be turned on or off independently. That is, they are not a device of drawing segments of straight lines as is seen on the "memory screens" or "refresh screens", for instance [1] [2] [3].

Workstations allowed one to use different windows on the screen simultaneously, and made possible the interactivity in the graphical input and output. Then the first standards for the screens started, workstation and other components of the hardware in graphic computing. The Geographical Kernel System (GKS) was the first ISO standard for low-level computer graphics, introduced in 1977 [6]. This system can be regarded as an access interface to the graphic peripherals, through a set of routines called by the user which would allow him to build a graphic application of an independent way from the specific terminal which was used at that moment. José Luis Encarnaçâo is one of the main founders and promoters of GKS, which was accepted as an international standard by ISO in 1982 [6].

In this historic framework it can be seen how graphic computing was focused from the start in a small environment of research and the academic and industrial development. In Southern Europe, the industrial engineers took the place of the graduates in sciences, physics, chemistry, mathematics, etc. and telecommunications engineers, electronic engineers, etc., for the technical questions, especially related to graphic hardware. With the passing of time, they also included within this hardware set the graphical software, but as a subset. Starting from the 90s the democratization of the software took place and when software was widened to the number of users in the world, costs reduction and the appearance of free software aimed at dynamic and/or static computer graphics [7]. Besides, with the goal of decreasing the interaction times between the users and the access to the databases and hyperbases, until reaching the brain-computer interfaces (BCIs) for communication and control (that is, interaction times, user-computer practically equal to a millisecond [8]. The brain activity produces electrical signals detectable on the scalp, on the cortical surface, or within the brain. Consequently, what is intended is an interaction of the user with the computer and its peripherals, without resorting to the movement of the arm muscles, the fingers, the voice, the eyes, etc. as it is generally done when working with the keyboard, mouse, microphone, eye movement readers, to mention some examples.

2   Interactivity and Communicability

Since the human being has had the chance to design the first set of pixels on a computer screen, the communication process between humans has changed for ever. Human communication is the alphabet of the progress of the societies since in it lies a whole wealth of knowledge and experiences that must be passed on to the future generations in a fast way, with restrained costs and in the best possible way. That is, by resorting to quality communication. In our case, communicability (figure 1).

Communicability in the current decade travels through an age of expansion thanks to the momentum of the Web, microcomputing, telecommunications and electronics, for instance [9]. However, today it is even easier to detect it in its absence than in its presence, especially in the contents of the static and dynamic media. In both media, audiovisual communication plays an essential role. Without forgetting the role of the text, basic in the evolution of the off-line hypermedia systems, and in the on-line net data, such as intranet, extranet and Internet. Systems that have made it possible to interact with the contents through the screen, the keyboard and the mouse. Without any doubt, the user's graphic interface has played an important role in the democratization of the CAD (Computer Aided Design) systems and CAM (Computer Aided Manufacturing) in the industrial environment, for instance.

Now there are several fields from which there has been an attempt to encompass the graphical interfaces issue. One of them and perhaps the one with the greatest circulation since 1989 has been usability engineering.[10], another the interfaces design sector, with a special stress on their programming and the universal criteria to be followed within the operating systems that worked in the Macintosh or with the IBM PC compatible under the Windows operating system. In this sense design guidelines were published, gaining a particular worldwide circulation the Apple "human interface guideline" [11] accompanied by other guidelines to understand the cultures of other peoples and thus avoid certain mistakes in the interfaces from the point of view of the icons, texts, colours, etc.

We can also mention the electronic-physical aspect of how to make up the pixel on a screen of the first computers that were of cathode rays (color), which synthetically can be depicted in the following way (figure 1 –bellow):

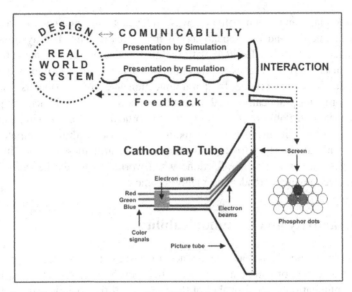

Fig. 1. Realism: Simulation and emulation. Classical representation of the human-interaction through a computer (color screen –cathode ray tube)

In this graphical representation are summed up the main technical aspects, which is usually the initial stage of that which is presented for the first time. At a later stage the interrelations between the technical aspects and the human being will be analyzed, that is, the intersections. Now communicability, in common with the origins of the multimedia notion, is not free of the lack of constraints and redundancy. Through a diachronic analysis some of the current communicability problems can be partially understood, by analyzing the multimedia notion.

From a linguistic perspective, the word multimedia entails some kind of redundancy. Etymologically, the "multi" prefix (which stems from the Latin "multi") means "many". The word "media" also derives from the Latin "medius" and inside a wide range of meanings is that which means: that it can serve for a given medium, quoting the case of communication. The word "multimedia" consequently cannot be regarded as a redundant notion, that is, the prefix "multi" added to the concept "media" does not increase its semantic value, since both are practically identical. Something similar happens with the expression "quality of communication" "quality of communicable" and "communicability".

That is, the intrinsic aspect of quality is searched for, even in accessibility notions of the information stored in the databases, the quality of the videogames or playability but which in an informal sense can be used to describe the ease by which the game can be played (that is, we mean one of the usability components enunciated by Jakob Nielsen in 1989 [10]), or the quantity or duration that a game can be played, in other words, the quality of gameplay. In this latter example the colloquial notion of language has been introduced which is different to scientific language, regardless of being applied to formal or factual sciences [11].

As a rule, when one speaks of a union or merger of areas of knowledge we are in the early stages of the research and the notions belonging to ICT (Information and Communication Technology) and must be anchored inside the relationship between meaning and signifier. Staying with with our example of the multimedia concept, this concept refers to the combination between themselves of two or more media, in turn made up by different support media. However, there are some who from the sector of the multimedia design systems already claimed in the 90s that multimedia is an intersection [13] [14] [15] and others that it is a union [16]. Such statements would not be incorrect if it is specified that in the case of the intersection we are talking about a communication process and in the case of the union of the technological aspect. Conklin [17] will later try to differentiate the decade of the 80s from the 90s in the multimedia environment by joining the word "interactive" to the word "multimedia", since the user in the communication process goes into a dynamic of constant feedback with the system through the navigation. The concept of navigation was the cornerstone of the research works in technological centres since 1970. Nicholas Negroponte and Richard Bolt developed a set of tools to increase the possibilities of interaction of the users with the computer [7].

These tools helped build the link between hypertext and interactive multimedia. They generated a working space called Dataland (data territory), whose main resources were the cursor, the touch system to manually interact with the screens, the joystick, zooming in, the use of the voice for the execution of the commands, among other things. The purpose was totally interactive multimedia. That is, that each source of information that was in digital format had a high degree of user-computer interaction. However, in this interaction process we can encounter a lack of transparency in the notions or lack of recognition towards the pioneers in certain academic sectors. An example of ambiguous definitions of communicability is to be found when it is claimed that it goes beyond the definition of the process, for this theoretical field responds to the practical fusion of four theoretical fields; perception, semiology, image rhetoric, and image syntax. That is, we have two different fields of the sciences, such as social psychology and semiotics (in Europe) or semiology (in the USA) of the image, mistakenly presented as four merged areas [18].

It is worth mentioning also the definitions deriving from the human-computer communication and the Human-Computer Interaction (HCI). HCI is a multidisciplinary area that studies the problems of usability of these interfaces [19]. Along time can be a myriad definitions deriving from the formal sciences and the factual sciences, without setting the limits of the fields of study, if we are talking about a union or an intersection of sets of disciplines, or the simple differences between multidisciplinarity and interdisciplinarity [20]. Until reaching unusual situations where some try to place the HCI as a subset of semiotics engineering, which is a theory to evaluate the communicability of the interfaces [21]. Obviously, this inclusion is totally mistaken as is the fact of turning semiotics into an engineering since this contradicts the main principles of science epistemology, for instance [12].

3   Social Sciences for a Hight Quality in Engineering

According to Basile and Musa [21], software engineering was going in the 90s through its quality golden era. From that field of engineering it was said that there was a need to insert professionals of the social sciences to increase the quality of the products and services that were brought forward by it, where the graphical interface of the user played a very important role, since, after all, they could either accept or turn down computer systems tailor-made for the management of industries, businesses, city halls, airports, etc. For instance, the presence of psychologists was necessary with regard to the cognitive models in the process of designing the elements that make up the interface, including the notion of metaphor for the interface [22]. That is, the importance of graphical computing for interaction was recognized, but there was a lack of ideal professionals in the multimedia field, for instance. Consequently, people talked colloquially but not scientifically about interdisciplinary work teams. The lack of differentiation at the time would result in myriad human mistakes from the university academic environment, with serious financial consequences for the ICT sector in the Southern Mediterranean until the present day. Those mistakes derive from human factors inside the engineering training and degrees belonging to the set of the formal sciences, especially when we are in the forefront of design for innovative products and/or services.

One of the genesis of those mistakes lies in the Southern Europe labour market, especially since the decade of the 90s, whether it is inside or outside the universities and research centres. They are trying to create qualified professionals in the latest technological breakthroughs in the least possible time, without caring about the research and development goals aimed at the innovative design and graphical computing in the long run. In the college research centres there should be a balance between theory and praxis of the new knowledge, the training of those professionals will always require a certain time. In those where the practice with commercial products beats the theory, only professionals are churned out, without motivation for research and aimed at commercial production. That is, we have super-specialists in narrows fields of knowledge, who lack a 360° vision to adapt to the constant changes deriving from microcomputing, for instance.

Moreover, they are not ready to face the new challenges of the future in the middle run. In that sense and inside the triad of our analysis the professionals from the colleges outside Europe are usually better prepared. They have better theoretical foundations in the formal and factual sciences. Another of the sources of those mistakes is due to the importation of working models alien to the academic environment, through which what many call knowledge and technology transfer between the business and the academic sector.

Theoretically this should be a bidirectional relationship, although the reality in the Mediterranean is sometimes unidirectional, from the business-industry (summit) towards the college (bottom). Obviously, in some geographical areas this can breed divergence rather than convergences, especially inside the work group of the new technologies aimed at innovative design resorting to CAD and the animated simulations in 2D and/or 3D. A classical example consists of dividing people between computer technicians and artists, in the framework of the computer animations, at the start and later on, to the multimedia, off-line and on-line, in some big Mediterranean cities, until it becomes a kind of fashion or model to be followed from the pedagogic point of view.

These antimodels were and are fostered by industrial engineers, computer science experts, fine arts graduates, etc., implemented in the audiovisual sector, belonging to public universities founded in the 90s. Antimodels which are also to be found in European private institutions related to design, art, multimedia, the audiovisual sector, the computer animations, virtual reality, etc.

In design innovation lies the industrial secret of the products aimed at the progress of humankind, especially if it is thought and made for the bottom of the world population pyramid. Not for nothing is it feasible to differentiate certain objects in relation to the decades, since all of them usually have a kind of common denominator among the components of the ensemble of that period. Sometimes these common features make that, out of commercial reasons and prompted by social and/or human factors, such as can be nostalgia or melancholy, for instance, they are reproduced again with that old style but with the latest technology available. Objects are motley, and they include from electronic engineering down to mechanic engineering.

A classical example are the cars belonging to the middle class of the European population. In the decade we are going through, the CAD applied to the industrial sector must be based on the concepts where ergonomy and nature coincide [24].

Therefore, new professionals are required, capable of moving in each one of the stages which are implicit in the making of innovative projects. The production should exclude the relationships with marketing in the design stage. Where these exist they should take a lower place than design and avoid publicity slogans related to pseudo creativity, such as: ideas manufacturer, innovator, originally provocative, among so many others, because a mistake in the 2D or 3D design may entail high costs in the production stage of an industrial chain. Besides, one thing is to carry out three-dimensional artistic objects, where the flaws may go unnoticed to the eye of the viewer as a component of the work. A classical example are the mistakes that can be seen in the 3D animation series for kids.

In the industrial design environment, accuracy is a rule to be respected. As Bruno Munari said [25], "one must observe a lot to comprehend the essence and carry out the solution fast". Moreover, in these three verbs lies the central axis of our design times. That is, "to observe" where the design can be applied in the context, "comprehend" is the essential moment to establish which is or which are the needs to be met and the requisites to be fulfilled with the solution and finally, "carry out" interdisciplinary knowledge should guarantee an efficient and efficacious project. To finish with these notions it is important to remember the decalogue of the good designer established by Dieter Rams [26] in the making of a project:

- A good design is innovating
- It generates sense and usefulness to a product
- It is aesthetical
- The product defines itself
- It is not invasive
- It is honest and sincere
- It is aimed at a long temporal duration
- It is consistent down to the smallest detail
- It respects the environment
- It resorts to the minimal possible design

These principles are present in those technological innovative products which are accepted by the whole population pyramid, a population pyramid which has one of its main vortexes in training. A training model that respects the principles and rules of pedagogy and progressive knowledge, constant and qualitative from the preschool age down to the training courses, post-university degrees, for instance.

Courses which may be aimed at sector professionals who want to get an update on techniques and programming methods, communicability strategies, the latest ergonomic improvements for interactive design, etc. aimed at vector animations in the small screens of the mobile multimedia and on-line microcomputing. All these professionals expect the courses they attend to respect the basic rules of teaching, which have built up their learning model.

4   Expansion of Antimodels

From academic environments that we may call antimodels for our triad, college courses, masters, updating seminars, etc. were organized from a clearly practical point of view, leaving the theoretical issues on the background. They focused on the technical aspects of commercial software. In this regard it is should be mentioned that two contradictory models were built, the students for workstation and the second group with PCs. The former built high level work with Softimage, Maya, etc., on Silicon Graphics workstations (1995), for instance. In figure 2 evolution of the computer PC and workstation in Europe [27].

That is, they required heavy investments of money and consequently the knowledge was aimed at a privileged elite of students. The latter, who worked with personal computers boosted from the hardware point of view for graphic computing (graphic cards, additional memories, disk space or in the net –intranet– for the storage of the animations, etc.) and with commercial products aimed at democratizing for ever graphic computing and computer animations with the software from Autodesk (AutoCAD, 3D Studio Viz, 3D Studio Max, etc.), for instance. In the 1990s and early 2000s some professionals belonging to the former group were able to see their productions reach the cinema. Whereas those in the latter group plumped for off-line multimedia, TV and the Internet.

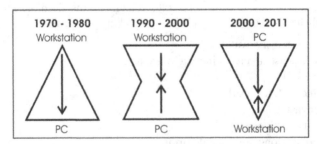

Fig. 2. History of the graphic workstation and PCs diffusion in Europe (the length of the arrows indicate which hardware predominated)

The high maintenance costs of the hardware and also the yearly renewal of software licenses are leading the animation producers for the digital media to the centre of the pyramid. Now this process hasn't been easy at all, especially for those who claimed that the quality of an animation could even be achieved without having high range graphic software and hardware available. It was a democratic process with some landmarks, such as making the users realize that it was possible to create pieces of static or dynamic graphic computing at home.

The secret of the communicability in computer animations aimed at the wide international audience always goes through four components interrelated among themselves in a bidirectional way: simplicity, universality, originality and humour. These are strategic components that should be transmitted to the future professionals of the sector in a fast and efficient way.

In the figure 3 [28] underlined is a clone computer, bolstered with graphic cards and commercial software for 3D (a very low cost compared with the workstation) joined to the knowledge of the traditional graphic arts (paper support), the software to generate vector images and bitmaps images, the special effects and the historical research (real contents, for example, the symbols of calendar Maya's), the results obtained were similar to the Silicon Graphics workstation. This image was a small experiment made in Sabadell, Spain (1995), thanks to the disinterested collaboration with two infographics technicians but which has meant a "before" and an "after" in the democratization process of the animated pixel in Spain.

The goal was to lend special interest to the users of the widest part of the pyramid, that is, the bottom, in order to motivate them towards the quality of interactive communication.

Fig. 3. This static image is a little (r)evolution in the history of democratization of the pixels in Spain: marketing (software and hardware) area, academic sectors: computer graphics, computer animation, and multimedia.

5   Animated Pixels in the Social Sciences and the Future Professionals

In some contexts of the college audiovisual environment in the Mediterranean basin, in the mid 90s and early 2000s the curricula were made quickly and in an inexperienced way by professionals of the formal sciences (industrial engineers, physicists, chemists, astronomers, etc.). These curricula had an area of new technologies, where the future professionals were included, in the learning of the animated pixels in quarterly subjects.

In fact those were subjects that forced the students to work without previous experience in the latest versions (in English) of Autodesk (AutoCAD, 3D Studio Viz, 3D Studio Max, etc.). This subject had as its main goal the making of a computer animation in 2D and/or 3D with a commercial software, whose commands were in English. There were some students in the group who were using a computer for the first time. That is, the access gap to the latest technologies in the population prompted the phenomenon that is currently known as "digital divide" [29]. Many of these users, even if they lived in big cities, with an important computer web, thanks to the ATMs in the banks, such as the city of Barcelona in the 90s, did not have a PC at home to carry out practice exercises, nor access to the commercial software for computer animations (nowadays thanks to the free software it is possible to find programmes for 3D such as Art of Illusion, 3D Canvas, K-3D, Make Human, DAZ Studio, etc.) nor the knowledge of technical English, etc.

Consequently, the works were finished by the professors of theory and practices (rendering, detection and correction of mistakes related to lighting, movement of the cameras, movement of the characters, etc.) Besides, with these potential computer users there was not only a problem in the usability engineering field with regard to the use of the computer, but also some other basic pedagogical factors had to be added, such as the foundations of graphic computing, the making of a storyboard until arriving finally at the making of animation proper. In short, a deviation of the college pedagogic reality deriving from the human factors in the formal sciences, which forced the students to multiply their efforts for passing the subject. The same happened with the multimedia, where the students of the early courses had to carry out off-line multimedia systems with Macro Media Director, for instance. Once again they resorted to the dogmas of the software engineering of the 90s, which consisted in making up interdisciplinary work groups, in our case for the animations. Inside those groups were those who were interested in the practices and others in the theoretical aspects, but related to the software to carry out the animation. That is, to split the tasks and the roles inside the group to unite and reach the common goal. A reality that, if we use the concepts of synchronism and diachronism deriving from linguistics, for instance, we find that the areas of technical teaching related to the computer animations, synchronically, were divided into several "small umbrellas" or sectors: computer animations, multimedia, virtual reality, digital sound or music technology, cognitive systems, cinema digital, video games, etc. Currently they are all united under the "beach or great umbrella" of the human-computer interaction. We have a schematic representation in the figure 4. That is, that all the subjects include the human-computer interaction as the panacea to reach the perfect interactive design, however, they leave communicability aside.

In the current decade, the idea rules of joining or merging all the branches of knowledge. Both positions are extreme and the balance lies in the intersection of the formal and factual sciences, such as the balance between theory and practice.

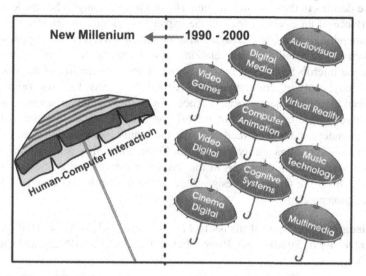

Fig. 4. In the 90s and beginning of the new century the division of practical knowledge was the prevailing factor in some educational centres of the audiovisual sector (i.e., Barcelona, Spain).

This simple synchronic and diachronic example makes apparent how the human factors with regard to the new generations may result in negative consequences for the professional future of the students, because they are experts in partial and temporal knowledge. Whereas if the theory is approached in the right way, even inside the graphic computing sector, it is useful to have timeless knowledge which can be easily adapted to the breakthroughs stemming from the software and the hardware. The curricula in our triad must be designed by real experts, tending to minimize to the utmost the social consequences, since sometimes in the figures coming from the statistic offices about joblessness, the mistakes come from the past, and especially from the educational or training sector of the working population [30] [31] [32].

6   Conclusion

Since Ivan E. Sutherland presented Sketchpad, computer graphics (hardware and software) has evolved in a breathtaking way, always trying to cut down the working times of the human being and the reaction of the computers with their peripherals. We have gone from fractions of a minute in the off-line multimedia systems in the late 20th century to a millisecond in the second decade of the 21st century through the brain-computer interfaces (BCIs) for communication control, with a huge potentiality in the static and dynamic means which contain graphics and for all the users, including those who do not have any disability in the arms or hands, for instance. In half a century we have seen the democratization process of the pixel, thanks to the usability in the Internet of the 90s, the right design of products and/or computer services, including the ergonomic aspect (hardware) and the communicability of the interactive designs in the new millennium. The diachronic analysis has made apparent the importance of an essential triad in the expansion era of communicability, that is graphic computing, interactive design and communicability. These components have among themselves a bidirectional relationship and require new professionals, who overcome the interdisciplinary teams of the era of software quality of the 90s. In our field of study, only a communicability expert who has had his origins in a communication environment (social sciences) including computer science, and later on going through the experiences of the off-line and on-line multimedia systems of the 90s can understand and correctly analyze the requirements of that triad in the era of expansion of communicability in our days. Communicability is always present to a greater or lesser extent in the pixels of the screens of our interactive systems and will be aimed at from the computer design stage in the least possible time and with the least production costs.

Acknowledgments. A special thanks to Maria Ficarra (ALAIPO & AINCI), Emma Nicol (University of Strathclyde), Pamela Fulton (ALAIPO & AINCI), and Carlos for their helps.

References

1. Newman, W., Sproull, R.: Principles of Interactive Computer Graphics. McGraw Hill, New York (1979)
2. Rogers, D.: Procedural Elements for Computer Graphics. McGraw Hill, New York (1985)
3. Lucas, M., Gardan, Y.: Techniques Graphiques Interactives et CAO. Gardan Hermes Publishing, Paris (1983)
4. Rosebush, J.: Historical Computer Animation: The First Decada 1960-1970. ACM Siggraph, New York (1992)
5. Ramamoorthy, C., Tsai, W.: Advances in Software Engineering. IEEE Computer 29(10), 49–58 (1996)
6. Hopgood, F., et al.: Introduction to the Graphical Kernel Systems GKS. Academic, New York (1983)
7. Cipolla-Ficarra, F., Cipolla-Ficarra, M.: Interactive Systems, Design and Heuristic Evaluation: The Importance of the Diachronic Vision. In: Tsihrintzis, G.A., et al. (eds.) New Direct. in Intel. Interac. Multimedia. SCI, vol. 142, pp. 625–634. Springer, Heidelberg (2008)
8. McFarland, D., Wolpaw, J.: Brain-Computer Interfaces for Communication and Control. Communications of ACM 54(5), 60–66 (2011)
9. Cipolla-Ficarra, F.: Quality and Communicability for Interactive Hypermedia Systems: Concepts and Practices for Design. IGI Global, Hershey (2011)
10. Nielsen, J.: Usability Engineering. Academic Press, London (1993)
11. Apple: Macintosh Human Interface Guidelines. Addison-Wesley, Massachusetts (1992)

12. Bunge, M.: The science: your method and your philosophy. Siglo XXI, Buenos Aires (1981)
13. Kjelldahl, L.: Collected Conclusions: Multimedia Systems, Interactions and Applications. In: Proc. First Eurographics Workshop. Springer, Stockholm (1991)
14. Väänänen, K.: Interfaces to hypermedia: Communicating the structure and interactions possibilities to the users. Computer & Graphics 17(3), 219–228 (1993)
15. Grimes, J., Potel, M.: What is Multimedia? IEEE Computer Graphics 1, 49–52 (1991)
16. Meyer-Wegener, K.: Database Management for Multimedia Applications. Multimedia, pp. 105–119. Springer, Berlin (1994)
17. Conklin, J.: Hypertext: An Introduction and Survey. IEEE Computer 20(9), 17–41 (1987)
18. Nöth, W.: Handbook of Semiotics. Indiana University Press, Indianapolis (1995)
19. Nielsen, J.: Designing Web Usability. New Riders Publishing, Indianapolis (2000)
20. O'Neill, S.: Interactive Media: The Semiotics of Embobied Interaction. Springer, Berlin (2008)
21. Cipolla-Ficarra, F., et al.: Advances in Dynamic and Static Media for Interactive Systems: Communicability, Computer Science and Design. Blue Herons, Bergamo (2011)
22. Basili, V., Musa, J.: The Future Engineering of Software – A Management Perspective. IEEE Software 24(9), 90–96 (1991)
23. Lévy, P.: La oralidad primaria, la escritura y la información. In: David, Goliath (eds.), vol. 58, Buenos Aires, Clacso (1991)
24. Cipolla Ficarra, F.V., Cipolla Ficarra, M., Giulianelli, D.A.: Industrial E-Commerce and Visualization of Products: 3D Rotation versus 2D Metamorphosis. In: Smith, M.J., Salvendy, G. (eds.) Human Interface, Part II, HCII 2009. LNCS, vol. 5618, pp. 249–258. Springer, Heidelberg (2009)
25. Munari, B.: Cómo nacen los objetos? Apuntes para una metodología proyectual. Gustavo Gili, Barcelona (2010)
26. Lovell, S.: As Little Design as Possible: The Work of Dieter Rams. Phaidon Press, London (2010)
27. Lamborghini, B.: European Information Technology Observatory. EITO-EEIG, Frankfurt (2001)
28. Cipolla-Ficarra, F., et al.: Arte Virtual. Autocad Magazine 36, 70–72 (1995)
29. Dijk, J., Hacker, K.: The Digital Divide as a Complex and Dynamic Phenomenon. The Information Society 19(4), 315–326 (2003)
30. Salas, C.: La crisis explicada a sus victimas. Altera, Barcelona (2009)
31. Pirolli, P., Preece, J., Shneiderman, B.: Cyberinfrastructure for Social Action on National Priorities. IEEE Computer 43(11), 20–21 (2010)
32. Miller, T., et al.: Engineering and Innovation: An Immersive Start-up Experience. IEEE Computer 44(4), 38–46 (2011)

Melody Generation Based on Thematic Development Method Using Pitch Class Set and Rhythm Complexity

Chih-Fang Huang[1] and Shu-Fang Ko[2]

[1] Department of Information Communication,
Yuan Ze University, Taiwan
jeffh@saturn.yzu.edu.tw
[2] Master Program of Sound and Music Innovative Technologies,
National Chiao Tung University, Taiwan
yeiamy.98g@g2.nctu.edu.tw

Abstract. This research is to create a melody generation system. Instead of using Markov chain with individual music parameter probability control, the pitch class set theory is adopted instead of generating pitch. The generated melody consists of motive and thematic development with variation. In addition rhythm complexity analysis technique is introduced in the proposed system with the inverse LHL method, to generate the rhythm with the rhythm complexity input automatically. This system can be used for algorithmic composition, and two cases have been verified successfully.

Keywords: Melody Generation System, Pitch Class Set, Motive and Thematic Development, Rhythm Complexity.

1   Introduction

Music generation using algorithms have been developed for decades, including Markov chain [1, 2, 3], evolutionary method [4, 5], etc. Based on algorithmic composition techniques and music theory understanding, some melody generators have been developed with dedicated interface to generate tonal melodies easily [6, 7]. In this system, the user has to choose the note number of prime form [8, 9], rhythm complexity, meter, and bar number, to dramatically reduce the complicated music parameter input, as shown in Fig. 1. Rhythm will be generated from complexity, and pitch will be generated from the prime form and its variations.

2   Motive and Thematic Development

Motive and Thematic Development is the basic idea to compose music, which includes both pitch structure and rhythm pattern. The following will depict the operations with examples.

F.V. Cipolla-Ficarra et al. (Eds.): CCGIDIS 2011, LNCS 7545, pp. 14–27, 2012.
© Springer-Verlag Berlin Heidelberg 2012

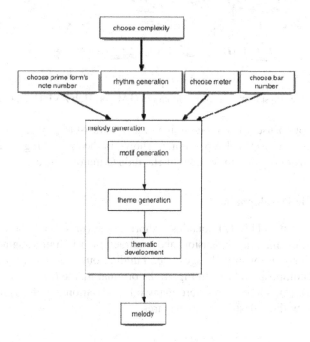

Fig. 1. System Diagram

2.1   Motive and Theme

A motive is a short musical idea which generally appears in characteristic and impressive manner at the beginning of a piece [10]. It consists of intervals and rhythms, and it is often considered as the 'germ' of the idea in music. Motive appears constantly throughout the whole piece which is used by repetition. The repetition may be exact, modified or developed.

Fig. 2. Motive

A theme is usually a complete phrase or period [10]. In the simplest case, the structure consists of an even number of measures; eight or multiple of eight

Fig. 3. Theme (First theme Haydn's Sonata in G Major, Hob XVI: G1, 1, mm. 1-12)

(i.e. 16, 32) is often used. If the beginning is a two-measure phrase, the 3rd and 4th measure may be a transposed repetition, as shown in the case of Fig. 2. Fig. 3 shows the first theme from the first movement of Haydn's G major sonata.

2.2   Thematic Development

Thematic development [11, 12] contains a short theme (or several short themes) and uses transposition, interval expansion and contraction, rhythmic augmentation and diminution, inversion, tonality changes, etc., building out of it a lengthy composition or section of a composition [11]. In Fig. 4, the original theme (a) varies in a few ways like (b), (c), (d), (e), and (f). There are many other variations on the same theme that might be varied without destroying its features.

Fig. 4. Thematic Development [11]

3   Pitch Class Set

A pitch-class set (PCS) uses integers p = {0, 1,..., 11} to represent the collection of pitches from the 12-tone chromatic scale [9]. It is an unordered collection of pitch classes, such as [0, 4, 7], using "modulo 12" to obtain the residue numbers from 0 to 11. It can be varied by "transposition", "inversion", and both of them. The prime form is considered to be the "simplest" version of the PCS. Some examples of PCS variation are shown in Fig. 5.

Original pitch class set : [0 1 5]

$[2\ 3\ 7] = T_2\ [0\ 1\ 5]$

$[0\ 7\ 11] = T_0 I\ [0\ 1\ 5]$

$[1\ 2\ 9] = T_2 I\ [0\ 1\ 5]$

Fig. 5. Examples of Pitch Class Set Variation

4   Rhythm Generation by Inverse LHL

Rhythm complexity analysis [13, 14] methods can be used to determine the complexity of the existing musical rhythm. In this paper the proposed rhythm generation is based on the inverse method of rhythm complexity analysis, based on the following paragraphs.

4.1   LHL Rhythm Complexity

LHL Rhythm Complexity analysis was derived by H. Longuet-Higgins and C. Lee [15], to designate the metrical unit from various levels of the rhythmic structure. The tree structure is used to represent the metrical hierarchy with each note weighted. More detailed description about the LHL implementation can be found in various literatures [16, 17].

LHL is the method to find rhythmic syncopation, based on the metrical hierarchy to determine the syncopated notes shown in the position of the measure. LHL will adjust the weight of metrical hierarchy, where 0 is the highest weight representing a completely unsyncopated rhythm, and the negative integers (-1, -2, ...) will decrease progressively to represent syncopated rhythms. LHL is based on the Western musical tradition of dividing music into musical rhythmic patterns followed the "measures" or groupings of pulses. The simple time is assumed in LHL, and the measure will be divided into the minimum unit, for example a quarter note in 4/4 time, and a tree diagram as shown in Fig. 4.1 can be determined with weights marked, "0" means the position divided by 1, "-1" means the position divided by 2, and so on. After all weights are marked, rest (.) and onset (x) position can be found out, and then compute the value of "rest" minus "onset"; if it is positive, then it refers to the syncopated position, as shown in Fig. 6. [18].

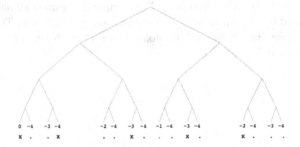

Fig. 6. Tree Diagram for the LHL Analysis of Musical Rhythm Complexity [18]

4.2   Inverse LHL Method

Since LHL is a good method to analyze the rhythm complexity, the proposed system attempts to use the inverse way to "compose" or "synthesize" music rhythm pattern to play the role of rhythm generator for the algorithmic composition [19]. Fig. 7 shows the tree structure of the LHL hierarchy with more detailed explanation.

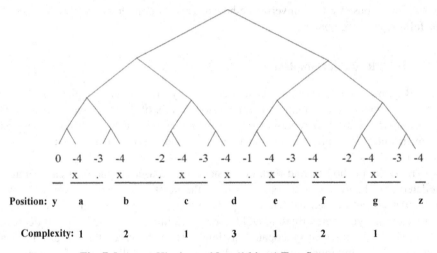

Fig. 7. Longuet-Higgins and Lee (16-baet) Tree Structure

- "x" is the onset position, and "." represents no onset which can be either rests or the fermata of "x".
- a, b, c, d, e, f, and g are the places that rhythm complexity shows up. It exists in the position where weight of "." subtracts from "x" weight if it is greater than zero.
- "-1", "-2", "-3", "-4" represents half note, quarter note, eighth note, and sixteenth note, respectively. "x" shows the position where complexity happens.

Various complexity values with their combinations are shown in Table 1:

Table 1. Complexity Combinations

The Complexity Value with Possible Combinations that the System Can Generate		Generation Method: (n) Represents to Select n of them
1	1	1
2	1+1	2
	2	
3	1+1+1	3
	1+2	
	3	
4	1+1+1+1	4
	1+1+2	
	2+2	
	1+3	
5	1+1+1+2	5
	1+1+3	
	2+2+1	
	2+3	
6	1+1+1+1+2	6
	1+1+1+3	
	1+1+2+2	
	1+3+2	
7	1+1+1+1+3	7
	1+1+1+2+2	
8	1+1+1+1+2+2	8
9	1+1+1+1+3+2	9
10	1+1+1+2+2+3	a.c.e.g (3) + b.f (2) + d
11	1+1+1+1+2+2+3	a.c.e.g (4) + b.f (2) + d

5   Melody Generation

After rhythm is generated, pitch will be generated, according to the user's selection of prime form number (from 3-note to 6-note), and a set of them will be selected randomly by the system as the motive's prime form. For instance, if prime form number 3 is selected by the system, then there are 19 prime forms that can be used randomly. A measure is considered as a unit, and four operations including prime series (P), transposition (Tn), and transposed inversion (TnI) can be used to generate the music motive, with integer number n randomly generated from 1 to 11, and pitch register randomly determined from C0 to C7, to generate pitches. The proposed melody generation process is as shown in Fig. 8.

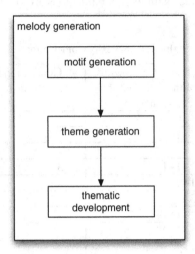

Fig. 8. Melody Generation Process

5.1   Motive Generation

A motive's length is usually two measures, and it is composed of intervals and rhythms. The motive's rhythm will be generated according to complexity (mapping different quadrants), and we use pitch class set theory to generate the motive's pitches.

5.2   Theme Generation

A music theme can be generated based on the motive operation. The following paragraphs will depict the detailed theme development.

5.2.1   Theme

A theme is usually a complete phrase or period [10]. We defined theme's length as 8 measures. Measure 1-4 is called "antecedent", and measure 5-8 is called "consequent". Consequent should be in part a repetition of the antecedent. The motive is 2-measures, its repetition and variation will appear in measure 5 and measure 6. The antecedent usually ends on V, and sometimes ends on I. The consequent usually ends on I, V or III (major or minor) with a full harmonic cadence. Fig. 9 shows the motive development for a theme with pitch-level and rhythmic operations. Note that there are no motives within measure 3-4 and measure 7-8, which are independent music elements.

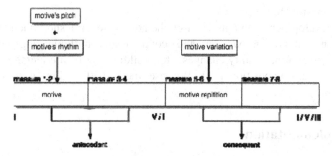

Fig. 9. Theme and Motive

5.2.2   Motive Repetition Method

A motive is used by repetition, including exact, modified or developed. Exact repetition means preserve all features and relationships, i.e. transposition, inversion, retrograde, diminutions and augmentation. Variation creates modified repetitions, it changes some features and preserves the rest [10, 20]. Fig. 10 is the example of motive repetition from Schoenberg's string quartet No. 4 using the above techniques.

Fig. 10. Motive Repetition Example
(Transposition and Inversion example from: Schoenberg's String Quartet No.4)

5.2.3   Thematic Development

Thematic development contains a short theme (or several short themes) and uses transposition, interval expansion and contraction, rhythmic augmentation and diminution, inversion, tonality changes, etc., building out of it a lengthy composition or section of a composition [11]. We use methods like Fig. 4 to do thematic development.

6   Implementation

In this paper a simple graphic user interface (GUI) is designed for the user to select meter, bar number, rhythm complexity, and the note number of prime form, as shown in Fig. 11. The system applies inverse LHL method to generate rhythm pattern, therefore various complexity values will generate the rhythm patterns randomly with the possible combinations. In the pitch-level consideration, pitch can be generated according to PCS theory. This melody generator can generate a piece of music with motive operation and thematic variations. Compared with the previous algorithmic composition methods, the proposed system can generate music with a unity and its variations, rather than randomly select pitches.

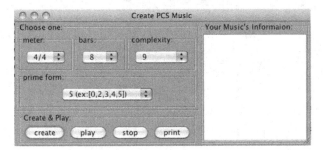

Fig. 11. System Interface

Fig. 12 is the flow chart of the software program, including the data input, process, and system output:

6.1   Meter

There are two kinds of meter that can be selected by the user, 3/4 and 4/4, to generate 3-beat and 4-beat music respectively. Due to the limitation of calculation, only 4/4 meter can be generated by the inverse LHL method, 3/4 meter is generated by the built-in rhythmic patterns randomly selected from the database so far.

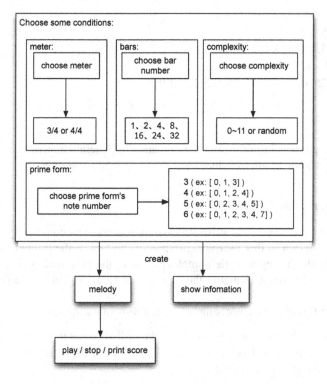

Fig. 12. The Flow Chart of the Software Program

The following database is based on our predefined patterns in 3/4 time, where 1.0 is quarter note, 0.5 is eighth note, and so on.

- {1.0, 1.0, 1.0},
- {1.0, 0.5, 0.5, 1.0},
- {0.5, 0.5, 0.5, 0.5, 0.5, 0.5},
- {0.5, 0.5, 0.5, 0.5, 1.0},
- {0.5, 0.5, 1.0, 1.0},
- {1.0, 0.25, 0.25, 0.25, 0.25, 0.5, 0.5},
- {1.5, 0.5, 1.0},
- {0.5, 0.5, 2.0},
- {1.0, 0.75, 0.25, 1.0},
- {1.0, 0.5, 0.5, 0.5, 0.5},
- {1.0, 2.0},
- {0.5, 0.5, 2.0},
- {0.5, 1.0, 0.5, 1.0},
- {0.5, 2.5},

- {2.5, 0.5},
- {-0.5, 0.5, 2.0},
- {-0.5, 0.5, 0.5, 0.5, 1.0},
- {-1.0, 0.5, 0.5, 1.0},
- {-0.25, 0.25, 0.25, 0.25, 0.5, 0.5, 1.0},

6.2   Bars

The music length equal to or greater than 8 bars will generate motive variation, and it needs at least 16-bar length to induce motive and thematic variation.

6.3   Rhythm Complexity

Using inverse LHL method to generate rhythm with various complexity values will influence the rhythm in this measure. In view of the fact of the limited variation for the generative rhythm by a single complexity value, the proposed system adds some notes in the beat without changing the complexity value, to enrich the rhythm with abundance.

The rule of filling add-on notes includes the following statement:

- If the randomized position is at "x", then fill all notes in the same unit.
- If the randomized position is at ".", and "x" in the same unit is not filled, then the system will fill it.

Different complexities will generate various rhythm combinations as shown in Table 4.1, and the system will calculate all the possible combinations based on the selected complexity value. The rhythm pattern within a measure can be randomly generated according to one of the generated rhythm combinations, and the duration of note and rest can be randomly generated too.

6.4   Pitch Generation

Pitch class set (PCS) theory is used to generate melody's pitch in this project. A Pitch-class sets use integers p = {0, 1,..., 11} to represent the collection of pitches from the 12-tone chromatic scale [9]. It is an unordered collection of pitch class, i.e [0, 4, 7], using "modulo 12" to a number from 0 to 11. And it can be varied by "transposition", "inversion", and both of them. The prime form is considered to be the "simplest" version of the pitch class set. When two prime forms produce the same interval vector, and when one cannot be reduced to the other (by inversion or transposition), they are said to be "Z-Related", or "Z Correspondents" [21]. We can find more possible prime forms from Z-relation, i.e. [0, 1, 4, 6] and [0, 1, 3, 7]. When the user chooses one prime form number from the interface, the system will random choose one prime form from the database, and the system uses "transposition", "inversion", and both of them to do variation. The prime form in the database of the proposed system is from 3-note (prime form number 3) to 6-note (prime form number 6), and the user can select one of them from the graphic user interface shown in Fig. 6.1.

7   Result

Two cases with various input conditions have been verified by the proposed system, and show the following result, and the selected prime forms, meter, bar number, and complexity is as shown in Table 2 and Table 3. Fig. 12 and Fig. 13 are the score output of the generated result, which shows a successful melodic generation based on the proposed method.

Case 1

Table 2. Input Condition for Case 1

Meter	4/4
Bar Number	8
Complexity	6
Prime Form	[0,3,5,6,8]

Fig. 13. System Result of Case 1

Case 2

Table 3.   Input Condition for Case 2

Meter	4/4
Bar Number	24
Complexity	Random
Prime Form	[0,3,5,7]

Fig. 14. System Result of Case 2

8   Conclusion

The proposed system is a melody generator which contains motive generation, theme generation and thematic development. The user has to choose prime form note number, complexity, meter, and bar number. Rhythm is generated based on complexity. Pitch class set theory is also used to generate most of the pitches as melody. Motive generation can be performed including the variations for rhythm and pitch, within a two-measure length. Theme generation involves one motive and its repetition, and also two harmonic cadences. Thematic development is done with the theme's variation. Two cases have been successfully verified by the melody generation system, which shows a better unity in aesthetics than the previous algorithmic composition, and hopefully the pitch class set and rhythm complexity based melody generator can be integrated with harmonic progression and counterpoint in the future.

Acknowledgment. The authors would like to appreciate the support from National Science Council projects of Taiwan: NSC99-2410-H-155 -035 -MY2.

References

1. Ames, C.: The Markov Process as a Compositional Model: A Survey and Tutorial. Leonardo 22(2), 175–187 (1989)
2. Cambouropoulos, E.: Markov Chains as an Aid to Computer Assisted Composition. Musical Praxis 1(1), 41–52 (1994)

3. Farbood, M., Schoner, B.: Analysis and Synthesis of Palestrina-Style Counterpoint Using Markov Chains. In: The International Computer Music Conference, Havana, Cuba, pp. 18–22 (September 2001)
4. Wiggins, G., Papadopoulos, G., Phon-Amnuaisuk, S., Tuson, A.: Evolutionary Methods for Musical Composition. In: Partial Proceedings of the 2nd International Conference CASYS 1998 on Computing Anticipatory Systems, Liège, Belgium, pp. 10–14 (1998)
5. Moroni, A., Manzolli, J., Zuben, F.V., Gudwin, R.: Evolutionary Computation applied to Algorithmic Composition. In: Proceedings of the 1999 Congress on Evolutionary Computation, CEC (1999)
6. Povel, D.J.: Melody Generator: A Device for Algorithmic Music Construction. Journal of Software Engineering & Applications 3, 683–695 (2010)
7. Temperley, D.: A Probabilistic Model of Melody Perception. Cognitive Science 32(2), 418–444 (2008)
8. Straus, J.N.: Introduction to Post-Tonal Theory. Prentice Hall, Englewood Cliffs (1990)
9. Schuijer, M.: Analyzing Atonal Music: Pitch-Class Set Theory and Its Contexts. Eastman Studies in Music 60. University of Rochester Press, Rochester (2008)
10. Schoenberg, A., Stein, L.: Fundamentals of Music Composition (1967)
11. Gehrkens, K.W.: The Project Gutenberg eBook, Music Notation and Terminology (2006)
12. Scruton, R.: The Aesthetics of Music. Clarendon Press, Oxford (1997)
13. Thul, E., Toussaint, G.T.: Rhythm complexity measures: A comparison of mathematical models of human perception and performance. In: Proc. 9th International Conference on Music Information Retrieval, Philadelphia, USA, pp. 14–18 (September 2008)
14. Shmulevich, I., Povel, D.-J.: Complexity measures of musical rhythms. In: Desain, P., Windsor, W.L. (eds.) Rhythm Perception and Production, pp. 239–244. Swets & Zeitlinger, Lisse (2000)
15. Longuet-Higgins, H., Lee, C.: The rhythmic interpretation of monophonic music. Music Perception 1(4), 424–441 (1984)
16. Fitch, W.T., Rosenfeld, A.J.: Perception and production of syncopated rhythms. Music Perception 25(1), 43–58 (2007)
17. Smith, L., Honing, H.: Evaluating and extending computational models of rhythmic syncopation in music. In: Proceedings of the International Computer Music Conference, pp. 688–691 (2006)
18. Thul, E., Toussaint, G.T.: Analysis of musical rhythm complexity measures in a cultural context. In: Proceedings of the 2008 C3S2E Conference (C3S2E 2008), pp. 1–9. ACM, New York (2008)
19. Cope, D.: The Algorithmic Composer, Madison, Wisconsin (2000)
20. Stein, L.: Structure & Style: The Study and Analysis of Musical Forms, Summy-Birchard Music (1979)
21. Nelson, P.: Pitch Class Sets, Revised on January 20 (2007), http://composertools.com/Theory/PCSets/ (accessed April 08, 2011)

Prolepsis in Computer Animation for Children

Francisco V. Cipolla Ficarra[1,2], Jacqueline Alma[3], and Miguel Cipolla-Ficarra[2]

HCI Lab. – F&F Multimedia Communications Corp.
[1] ALAIPO: Asociación Latina de Interacción Persona-Ordenador
[2] AINCI: Asociación Internacional de la Comunicación Interactiva
Via Pascoli, S. 15 – CP 7, 24121 Bergamo, Italy
[3] Universidad Nacional de La Pampa, Argentina
ficarra@alaipo.com, jacqueline_alma@yahoo.com, ficarra@ainci.com

Abstract. We present the importance of the prolepsis to analyze the animations for the future generations of users of interactive systems, starting from those that are broadcast in the audiovisual media. The main aspects of attention and motivation of the kids are studied, through the 3D characters and the need to count on experts in communicability to increase the quality of the contents in the Digital Terrestrial Television (DTTV or DTT) and the on-line and off-line multimedia systems. The results of a heuristic analysis of communicability in the different animation techniques for children are also presented.

Keywords: Behaviour Computer Animation, Education, Communicability, Computer Graphics, Multimedia, Evaluation.

1   Introduction

In the history of human communication, one of the main goals has been to beat the passage of time. Since the caves where primitive man drew the basic elements of his daily life, until the Persian, Egyptian, Aztec, Mayas, Incas eras, etc. there have been several supports that have allowed us to see historical drawings in our own era. In them, knowledge and experiences were transmitted for the present and future generations. These drawings, little by little, were incorporated into the communication social media of the early 20th century, with cinema as a main medium of national and international communication. In principle, the information load of these cartoons was aimed at the adult public. Later on, it was aimed at child and adolescent audiences. Implicitly there was a attempt to widen the public up until the present time, where computer animation techniques in tandem with traditional animation have as their main goal the children and teenager population. The purpose is to make the use of microcomputing in interactive multimedia systems something natural at the moment of having access to free access to content, as has been traditional with tv for the "monomedia generation" in the last decades of the 20th century [1]. Making a first diachronic analysis, considering the size of the screens and the reception-interaction systems of broadcast we have three groups of audiences at the moment of of having access to multimedia contents in the last two decades: the monomedia generation, the

F.V. Cipolla-Ficarra et al. (Eds.): CCGIDIS 2011, LNCS 7545, pp. 28–41, 2012.
© Springer-Verlag Berlin Heidelberg 2012

traditional multimedia generation and the microcomputing multimedia generation. In the first group you can place users whose age is above 60, in the second users in the 35-59 bracket. The remaining users make up the third group. Within the third group there are two subsets of potential users whose ages oscillate between 3-6 years and 7-10 years where the prolepsis is oriented in our field of study. Both age ranges in the subsets are flexible since they are in relation to the sex of the users, their geographical location and the endo-culturalization and transculturalization factors [2] [3] [4], to name just a few variables.

In the context of computer animations for children, spread in both the dynamic and static means, including the enculturation and acculturation process in which they are involved, we find in the notion of prolepsis [5] an interesting analysis environment for the future generations who will interact with on-line and off-line interactive systems [6]. This gives the possibility of getting ahead of time, thanks to the resources stemming from the design structure of the interactive systems. In the case of our study we focus on four categories that make up the design of the animations; the presentation, the structure, panchronism and the content under the perspective of communicability. A communicability which may be considered as a double prolepsis, not only for the simple fact of knowing the techniques that allow one to anticipate the evolution of a storyboard, but also because the potential users are being trained, who once they reach adulthood will interact with multimedia systems with a greater complexity than the current ones. In the current work we start with an analysis of the financial factors that boost the division of the populations with regard to the access to the new technologies and the need to multiply the transparency in the dynamic and static media related to the audiovisual and the on-line and off-line interactive systems. Later on, the main differences from the point of view of the emulation and simulation of reality are explained and also the attention and the motivation in the context of children's animations, especially focusing on 3D computer animations which are broadcast on digital television in Italy. Our field of study focuses on the RAI YoYo channel for children during the first semester of 2011 (www.raiyoyo.rai.it). Also the reusability of the information in the animations is analyzed and the main technical aspects in the construction of the heads of the characters. At the end of the paper, we present a table with the results obtained in the heuristic assessment of computer-made TV series in 3D format for child audiences.

2   Financial Factors versus Transparence Multiplies

The financial factors and, indirectly, the lack of knowledge of the professionals who participate in the development of the devices, as well as their multimedia contents, increases the digital split of the population, that is, those who can have access to the latest technological breakthroughs and those who due to several social reasons have stayed anchored in the technological rearguard. The technological rearguard in the digital division is due to the fact that this sector of the national or international population must cover partially or totally the three daily priorities from the financial point of view: food, shelter and clothing [7]. Within the avant-garde group with the consumption of products and/or microcomputing services, one can currently see a tendency on behalf of those ICT (Information Communication and Technology) professionals in generating content and multimedia devices aimed at our study group, especially in childhood. As a rule, these are professionals who make an effort to belong to the pedagogical and/or design context of the multimedia systems, carrying out empirical research with their children, friends or classmates. That is, the results of these research works usually lack scientific value, although they belong to the field of audiovisual, usability engineering, software engineering, human-computer interaction, etc.

An expert in communicability can quickly detect the veracity of the scientific results on the basis of the principle of "transparency multiplies" versus "digital divide". "Transparency multiplies" is a first set of techniques and heuristic methods that intends to measure with great accuracy the factors that differentiate the on-line information, for instance.

Through the computer screens of the computers and the design of the interactive systems, among other variables, it has been possible to divide the users of the multimedia systems on-line and off-line. In contrast, in the animations of the evolution of the cinema language and TV audiovisuals, joined with the technological breakthroughs in both media, there has not only been a convergence towards the computer audiovisual sector, but it has boosted it. In the current animations for child audiences we can see endless series produced in many countries, with their different styles and where the techniques of the manual and traditional drawing are combined with stop-motion and 2D and/or 3D computer animations, just to mention a few examples.

In those animations that are aimed at the youngest users, one can see a strong teaching presence in the shapes, colours, numbers, position of the objects, etc. In some cases it is easily detectable how there has been a switch from the techniques and software instruments to carry out computer animations, such as the special effects. Obviously and just as in the first animations the great goal was to reach the big screen, that is, the cinema (the interested reader can consult the provided bibliography to understand the evolution between the intersection and union of the different animation techniques, hardware and software). However, with computers and the momentum of the off-line and then on-line multimedia, many animators have bet on the new technologies, starting by knowing the potential of the computer since the hand-made drawing, the colouring of the characters in the storyboard down to the lighting techniques in 3D and the retouching of the frames with programs for the editing of images and/or pictures such as Photoshop, for instance.

All of these breakthroughs in the computer-assisted design sector, self-editing, control quality of the animations, etc. have benefited the final quality of the audiovisual products for children. Especially with those digital professionals who have aimed their creations towards television, going through the multimedia systems. We find a classical example in the animations made in plasticine for child audiences such as Pingu (www.pingu.net –figure 1), an animated series which from the television screen went to the CD-ROM [8] and later on came back to television, with an innovative and enriched style for the child audience, with the aim of targetting the second subset of study in the current work. It is easy to detect in the different chapters of the series the incorporation of elements coming from digital animation, attempts at emulation of this with plasticine, such as waves on a waterhole on the ice. In some ways there is also an attempt to achieve the simulation of reality for kids.

Fig. 1. Animations made in plasticine: Pingu is a clasical and excellent example

3   Animations for Children

The concepts of animation and simulation are not synonymous in the current work [9] whether we are referring to the interfaces or the images in the static or dynamic sense of the animations, for instance. It is also important to remember that the animation mistakes for this kind of audience generally go unnoticed. However, in the different information supports used along two decades for Pingu and which have been studied in the current work, the communicability has always been excellent.

One of the advantages of using the resources of the digital dynamic means is that the clay animations increase the communicability in for example the details in the characters, the scenery, the camera movements, the humanization of the characters of the animal world, etc. It is easy to observe in the last episodes of the series Pingu, the lighting atmospheric effects, the close-ups showing the teeth or the penguin's eyes, the body transformations (lengthening, flattening, rounding, etc.) That is, the incorporation of the special effects generates an additional wealth to the storyboard, if they are compared with the first chapters broadcast on TV (the first was on the 26th of May of 1986), with those of the new millennium, for instance. In the last we can see that Pingu has grown and new characters have been incorporated to the series. In other words, the stop-motion animation, generally made with clay or another malleable material, which belongs to the group of "claymation", has benefited from the digital breakthroughs for the emulation and simulation of reality. This is a first conclusion drawn after analyzing the animation of more rigid objects, such as the children's series. Fireman Sam, in the classical version of this series of the 20th century (1985) compared with that of the 21st century (2004) just to mention an example.

Now the use of the digital media in the animations is not always synonymous with a high communicability. An example is the Spanish series of three-dimensional Spanish animation series for the youngest kids (Nani-Gugu, 2008 –www.pataboom.com). In it two childish characters interact, one from the Earth (Gugu) and another an extraterrestrial (Nani) who communicate the activities to be carried out through three riddles of objects that Nani makes in a cloud and Gugu brings in a small cart. From a technical point of view we are in the face of an excessive use of the reusability of information, such as the repeat of the same sentences, gestures and movements, special effects, objects, etc. (something that doesn't happen in the animations made with claymation).

There is, though, a minimalist design in these three-dimensional digital productions with the purpose of focusing the attention of the kids, broadcasting a series of episodes in a consecutive way, there is some kind of boredom and consequently a loss of interest of the child before the television screen, not only because of these repetitions, but also to a palette of scarcely joyful or warm colours (use of secondary colours in grey tones instead of primary colours, for instance), the rigidity of the characters in the movements that emulate the animation, stop-motion and objects they have to guess but which not all the kids of a large city have within their reach. That is, the entropy of communication is missing with the potential enjoyers of these television contents, a failure that can be transferred to the users of the interactive systems, if these series are transferred into on-line and/or off-line multimedia systems games.

3.1   Reusability of the Animation and Children Motivation

The failures of communicability in the audiovisual, we can also see it in the interactive systems because they make up the structural cornerstone of animation: shapes and behaviour of the characters, disposition of the objects in the scenery, colour range, lighting sources, special effects, etc. Although the reusability of the information in the computer animation allows to cut down costs, the abusive use of certain resources inside an animated story may end up by alienating the viewer or user of the screen, even those with a very young age.

Something identical happens with the Spanish series Zumbers (for the learning of numbers from 1 to 20 –www.motionpic.com), also computer-made, with an excellent graphical quality, because of the wealth of colours it contains (primary and secondary) and the five three-dimensional characters, of a great corpulence, such as an elephant, a rhinoceros, a hippopotamus, etc.

These characters have the task of carrying out a route among different points which at the end make up an object or animal (unveiled with fireworks until reaching the number 20). The repetition of the gestures, of the characters as each one of the numbered balloons is released, can also saturate the attention of the kids and even frustrate them, because the objects they discover are not available to them, such as can be an analog phone, a wind-up alarm-clock, etc.

This is one of the great communicability aspects deriving from the design of objects and even icons for multimedia phones which do not match daily reality, since they are stored in some museums that tell about the daily life of the early and mid 20th century. Besides, in the series "Zumbers" we can come across serious mistakes that contradict the main goal of said series: learning to count. In the locution in Italian of episode 41, at the end of the 20 points and once all the balloons have been thrown to the sky, two plums are uncovered, but in the translation you hear "one plum". Mistakes like these show that the quality control in the audiovisual contents for the kids can be equal to zero, even in productions directly or indirectly subsidized by the autonomous governments inside the EU (Generalitat de Catalunya). Another television series which uses in a recurrent way information reusability is "Boom & Reds". In it some tiny red characters, similar to fungi (www.motionpic.com) will shape objects that a pink giant flute player will always get wrong when he tries to guess them, even having someone who whispers clues to his ear. This adult's mistakes seem very funny to the tiny characters, until at the third attempt the giant finally guesses the object. This series has a lesser communicability (43%) as compared with the Zumbers series.

The children audience consumer of computer animations in the television series is similar in many occasions to an inexperienced user in the use of multimedia systems, when these encounter a point of information for the first time in a museum. The purpose is to know beforehand what he can see, following a linear route. We have this linearity of the message in the interactive systems in a sequence of frames and links in a unidirectional or bidirectional way, which make up a guided link, for instance. In Nani-Gugu or Zumbers they are unidirectional storylines with zero surprises for the viewer, except the problem posed (what activity the extraterrestrial Nani wants to develop) and the end (discovery of the hidden element in the route through the 20 points that make it up in Zumbers). Apparently, the child audience can follow the development of only a single story [10] [11] [12].

Evidently, the designers of these animations make a crass mistake, voluntary or not, by marginalizing the sector of the off-line interactive systems to which the kids have access from an early age, where it is feasible to carry out several activities simultaneously, such as the interactive systems based on the character Pingu and his family in the late 90s, for instance, with over 10 activities to be developed by the kids, whose ages go between 3-6 years [8]. Consequently, the computer animations for the infantile audience should incorporate a main action and several secondary actions.

An excellent example in our universe of study has been the television series Loopdidoo (www.loopdidoo.com), integrally made in 3D. In it, it is easy to see an excellent communicability and a very high quality level from the point of view of the animation script, the final quality of the images in the rendering, the special effects, the main and secondary characters, etc. All of that linked to the possibility of developing some mini-stories parallel to the main action. The attention and the motivation of the kids, and of the adult audience, who are in front of the TV screen is high. In some way you break the age barrier due to the aesthetic effect of the images [13] [14], for instance.

Images of natural objects such as trees, clouds, etc., come from 2D shapes to which later on the "z" coordinate is incorporated, and this makes all of them converge on an original environment, where the main and secondary characters of the mini-series are. Further the excellent choice of the textures, camera shots, the different kinds of lighting, among so many other components of the animation should be stressed. Many of them belong to the static set of the components (colours, pictures, textures, etc.)

and they acquire a special interest for the viewers, thanks to the speed in which the main story develops, including the secondary ones.

In contrast to what happens in the two already mentioned Spanish series, whose manifest goal is the learning of numbers, shapes, objects, etc. keeping a single story, linear, unidirectional and even monotonous, in Loopdidoo we have a special example from the point of view of movement and the storyboard.

Fig. 2. Prolepsis in computer animation for children: Loopidoo is an excellent example

The computer animation series Loopidoo, the fast but balanced rhythm between the animation and the interaction of the characters among themselves and/or elements of the scenery, makes viewers keep their attention until the last second, even in the final credits, when the final request of the fleas family who inhabit Loopidoo is shown. In some way we have the set of the traditional structure in three parts of the main story with small parallel subsets which allow to reach or not the main goal or serve to constantly draw attention to elements such as the microworld of these fleas. We are in an interesting case of narrations in parallel for the children audience. Graphically this can be depicted as a water wave with several peaks (introduction, conflict or problem to be solved climax and denouement of the conflict or problem), inside a sinusoidal movement, that is, the projection of the circular movement, also with beginning, development and ending, of a lesser duration in time [12]. These ellipses depict the mini stories inside the main plot. This level of perfection can only be reached in the short, middle and long term for potential local and international audiences in those computer animations where in the design stage the communicability professionals are incorporated . In other words, you get a final product that under the label of a kid audience may include in its fruition all the members of the family.

3.2   Computer Animation and Focus of Attention for Children

The new modalities entail generating several resources to draw and keep the attention of the viewers since an early age. In this sense it can be seen that the new generations have a distributed attention and they can easily focus on aspects of the layout (images) rather than on the texts (static or dynamic) and the audio. Hence there are three-dimensional characters who draw the attention of the childish viewer so that he carries out physical activities (jump, clap, etc.) or shares part of the dialogue with them, trying to get them involved in the development of the story. Obviously a specialised adult audience can detect these pedagogical recourses which boost the growth of the kids. However, the problem becomes even stronger in the animated series which are made by inexperienced animation technicians or without the financial resources to hire the services of pedagogues, for instance.

On the other margin, we have those professionals of the formal sciences (nuclear engineers, industrial engineers, chemistry graduates, mathematics, etc.) who resort to their children, friends, nursery schoolmates or of the elementary school to carry out experiments related to the design and/or intersection with the interactive systems in the communicability area, whose results from the point of view of epistemology of the sciences are hardly valid, especially when there is a wish to include the factual sciences within the framework of the formal sciences [15].

The pedagogy in the 2D and 3D computer animation should be controlled by real experts, backed by decades of experience and/or training, since the educational basis that starts in preschool education is at stake. A preschool education that, since the first institute was founded in 1816 in Lanark (Scotland), by the pedagogue Robert Owen has showed itself to be essential for the enculturation and transculturation processes of the adults to be [3] [16]. Although the age of the kids from which they start to attend may vary between 3 and 6 years, it is there where they learn how to communicate, play and interact with the others properly. Also these positive results can be accompanied by a children television programming that goes with them in this period of their lives. The teachers offer them several materials to manipulate and carry out activities that prompt them to learn the language and the vocabulary, mathematics, sciences in general, art, music, foreign languages, computer science and social behaviour. In few words, the new generations must consolidate the knowledge acquired in real life with those that are virtually presented on a TV screen and/or computer, regardless of their size.

Having kids as potential viewers and/or users of interactive systems has both positive and negative aspects inherent to the design. A negative aspect for the inexperienced professionals in the field of animations is achieving an excellent communicability in the least possible time, and with low costs, especially in the era of communicability expansion. In contrast, the positive aspect is that the computer allows to considerably reduce the production costs and even avoid legal issues related to the copyright issued in the early last century, but still in force in some countries of the EU, as is the Italian case in the matter of cultural heritage [17].

The production costs of TV series whose chapters have the same duration have a lower cost in case they are made with a computer as compared to the traditional animation done in clay, for instance. In this latter case the continuous movement is achieved by photographing every photogram where the characters shift their position, including all the elements that make up in a steady or dynamic way the rest of the scenery. That is why films like Chicken Run or Wallace & Gromit, a Matter of Loaf or Death (www.aardman.com), sometimes require a much longer production time than digital animation. Sometimes a time that may be similar to other projects of the financial industry in the computer animation, with the exception that once the characters are created in the computer, these can be quickly used in the later versions.

Something which is practically impossible with clay and requires an endless series of models because of the continuous transformations of the body and the face expressions. In this sense, we have seen how in the children television series that have gone through the interactive multimedia systems the characters have gained in expressivity and wealth in the emulation and simulation of reality where they are immersed. Without any doubt, the expressivity of most of the animated characters in 3D for the children audience focuses on the head (face) and especially the eyes. Those readers who want to go deeper into the movement issue of the eyes can look up the following bibliographic reference.

4   Minimalistic Style for Children

Having a child audience as the final destination of the computer animation productions has the advantage of working with simple characters, where it is not necessary to animate with a high level of realism those elements where are focused endless movements such as the hands or human hair. Although the commercial animation software incorporates the latest breakthroughs in algorithms of graphic computing which go from modelling towards the diverse lighting techniques, for instance, many 3D children's characters are minimalistic from the point of view of design. Nor do the climate effects require special attention or development of "ad hoc" applications to solve the problems deriving from situations such as the wind among the plants, the snow when it touches water surfaces, frozen or not, etc. In this regard, computer animation technicians will be responsible for applying and testing several options, within a margin of time and the parameters received from the head of the audiovisual or interactive production.

In relation to the experience of said technicians it is possible to cut down the production costs, since the commercial software for animations contains a high number of variables that can be similar among the different brands. For instance, the libraries of textures with the effect of the passing of time in bitmap images imply not having to use self-editing programs to generate those effects such as the combination of smoke and fire in a single special effect. The daily evolution of the graphic software and the hardware allows one to incorporate new options to decrease the production time and hypothetically the final costs, which sometimes can be increased because of the human factors underlying in everything related to the software quality [1]. The experience of the animator and the team's decisions allow one to choose between different techniques for the facial animation of the 3D characters, in relation to the available graphic software and hardware. The first thing is to determine the shape of the head and whether the elements that make it up are 100% subject to it or not. For instance, we can have animals whose eyebrows are floating and which allow it to gain expressivity in a short shot, to draw the user's attention. However, sometimes, not having these elements subject to the face and following the storyboard may be a costly option, given the complexity in certain scenes; lighting changes, atmospheric effects, interaction with other characters, etc. You also have to decide the basis of the head, that is, whether we generate it from zero or it comes from a 3D scanning, real or from a sculpture, for instance [18].

Once the scanning has been made, it is necessary to cut down the number of polygons that make up the obtained model. If we use flexible curves, first the curves will have to be adapted to the surface of the model, which will serve as a template to rebuild the whole model with flexible curves. Finally, we will discard the original polygonal structure of the model. Another way to generate the heads of the characters is to work with spheres since from the topological point of view a head may be considered as a deformed sphere. That is, we can place the sphere in such a way that the "north pole" (figure 3) is to be found on the upper part of the head (A), in the front (B) or on the sides (C). Each one of these positions has its pros and cons. A graphic representation is the following:

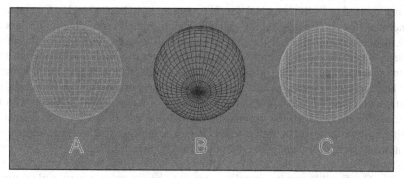

Fig. 3. Different techniques for the facial modelling of the 3D characters

If the "north pole" is on the upper part of the head (A), it makes the curves flexible in such a way that it does not match the alignment with the face muscles, which may make animation more difficult. In the case of using the frontal part (B), that is, that the "north pole" is to be found on the mouth, it makes the flexible curves to flow in a natural way along the same radial lines as in the mouth muscles, thus generating a simple and soft mouth animation. The problem arises at the moment of modelling the eye sockets, because the orientation of the flexible curves may be misadjusted or misplaced. Lastly, when we place the "north pole" at the height of the ears (C), they allow a better filling of the skin for modelling. That is, we have the flexible curves with a better orientation for the eyes sockets and the nostrils, but they are parallel to the mouth muscles. In spite of this, it is the best orientation in the case one chooses this modelling technique for the head.

Another technique that the designer may follow to generate the head of the characters is the technique of addition and subtraction [18]. It consists of slowly generating each one of the components of the face in an isolated fashion and then matching each one of them. One of the drawbacks is the high number of polygons that is generated and the later slow-down of the rendering process, for instance. In rounded faces we may resort to metaspheres, which generate smooth surfaces. Some of them have the function of addition to the main spheres such as fro example the cheeks, and others are from subtraction, like those that are in the area of the eyes cavity or the mouth, for instance.

Once the basic shape has been obtained with the jaw, the chin, the cheeks, ears, etc., one can insert the objects that will be animated, such as the eyes, eyebrows, lips, etc. The movement of the lips, showing teeth, tongue, etc., is a complex area to animate. However, in the children's animation context we may come across 3D series in which the characters have an "x" as a mouth, as it is the case of "Musti, the little cat" (created by Ray Goossens in 1945 –www.musti.be).

So far some techniques and methods have been enumerated whose speed in generating the model will depend on the experience of the computer animator. Evidently, there are other techniques such as covering with skin to realise the head, that is, sculpting the head from a series of silhouettes or shapes [19]. There is also the alternative of flat patches, giving them the shape of a face and adjusting to a faceless skull, as if it were a mask from a carnival, hiding the seams under the hair or behind the ears, that is, places where the head doesn't have any movement. In the first case – covering with skin – this is ideal for 3D animations where the characters have a symmetrical face, consequently, the animator can place the north pole in the ears and start with the accumulation of the skin in several silhouettes until half of the face is complete. Later on, the other half is a duplication operation and a 180° degrees twist until the other half of the face is achieved, thus considerably reducing the elaboration time. The three-dimensional character Uki (he is the personification of a toddler – www.ukiland.com), his friends and some elements of nature could be made with this technique, for instance. In the second alternative, the use of the patches consists of resorting to one or a set of flat patches. It is a technique that is more used in the animations of series for teenagers rather than for younger children.

Currently it is easy to detect when a head is made from flexible curves or with polygons. The flexible curves or splines are for characters that have a skin surface which emulates the human one. With them it is easy to keep a surface smooth since they define a soft skin with a much smaller number of vertexes than the polygonal models. The model with splines is minimalism par excellence, that is, less is more from the technical point of view in this case, because the simplicity of the described models allows a greater ease in the animation. Each time that a vertex point is incorporated, an additional spline, etc., one must evaluate very carefully which is its function before doing it. It can also be detected when the facial features in the heads of the children's characters are painted, that is, one can resort to animated texture maps. This technique makes modelling easier, since the maps (animated and hand-drawn or obtained from libraries) contain all the details. However, it entails an implicit slow-down at the moment of joining a 2D animation with the 3D movement of the body. Now the rhetorical question that it is necessary to solve when animating the dialogue of children's film characters is: Is it better to animate first the face or the body? The dialogue affects the whole character [20]. We have an excellent communicability when the whole body of the character comes into action at the moment of the dialogue. Now in the traditional animations the mouth of the characters was left until the last moment, that is, the body was done first. In the clay stop motion animations the mouth and the body can be animated simultaneously. Clearly there are some who prefer to animate the mouth before it interacts with other characters and the context, since it is easier to work with a still head than with a moving one. Another reason to make first the facial animation is to get the rhythm of the movie shot. This allows one to animate the body much better because it knows where the accents are deeper. The great exception is when children's film characters have very stressed gestures, such as talking with their hands, typical of the Latin peoples. Consequently, the answer to the rhetorical question depends on the storyboard, the main/secondary characters, and the decisions of the production team in relation to the available budget.

5   Evaluation: Results

The advance of computer animations can be seen in television programming for kids. In our case, we have also included those series that use stop-motion animation. The results where communicability and prolepsis are joined in the four analyzed design categories: presentation or layout (combination of colours, quality of the rendering, special effects, etc.), structure of the story (possibility of anticipating the characters' behaviour and within a context due to the repetition of the movement of said characters –reusability of a set of frames in the animation, for instance), panchronism (synchronization between audio and movement of the main facial components of the characters, movement of the rest of the body and of the elements that make up the scenery, for instance, thunder and lightning, explosions and smoke, etc.), and content (way of developing the action when it is known beforehand the behaviour of the characters, an oddity or the elements of nature, for instance, the transition from day to night, with the appearance of the moon and the stars on the sky). Graphically:

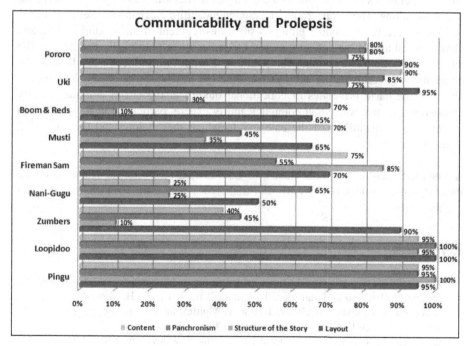

Fig. 4. The series TV with an excellent level of communicability and prolepsis are Loopidoo, Pingu, Uki and Pororo –the little penguin

The results obtained make apparent the excellent communicability quality of some children's animation series in Northern Europe that use stop-motion animation techniques, for instance. This is due to the high quality and originality of the content. In contrast, the repetitive use of frames in 3D animation, in children's series that have a didactic purpose and that are computer-made in Southern Europe, considerably decrease the viewers' prolepsis and may damage the motivation towards the interaction of the interactive systems in adulthood.

6   Conclusion

The dynamic media are excellent for boosting the attention and motivation towards the new technologies from an early age, as has been demonstrated in the computer animation in the videogame European industry in the last two decades. The essential requirement that must be met by the current computer animations, in a explicit way from the design stage onwards, is communicability. The different ways of generating these 3D animations make apparent that the new generations are from a very early age exposed to worlds that emulate and simulate reality on screens. These are screens which decrease in size and gain in freedom of fruition, as the age of the viewer and/or user of the interactive systems increases. Although the cost of the new interactive devices increases the digital divide among the population, the previous knowledge and/or experiences of those who make computer animations can negatively affect the new generations. They must know the communicability mechanisms well, especially because we are facing double prolepsis situations (content of the dynamic media and chronological age of the potential users of the interactive multimedia systems). In the current study animations made in Southern Europe with direct subsidies of the autonomous governments or indirect from the EU have been detected which do not abide by the basic principles of educational quality in the era of communicability expansion. It is necessary that communicability experts participate in the production of animations, regardless of the category to which they belong and the animation techniques used.

Acknowledgments. A special thanks to Luis Garcia (Universidad Nacional de La Pampa), Emma Nicol (University of Strathclyde) and Carlos for their helps and collaboration.

References

1. Ficarra, F.V.C., Ficarra, M.C.: Computer Animation and Communicability in Multimedia System: A Trichotomy Evaluation. In: Damiani, E., Jeong, J., Howlett, R.J., Jain, L.C. (eds.) New Directions in Intelligent Interactive Multimedia Systems and Services - 2. SCI, vol. 226, pp. 103–115. Springer, Heidelberg (2009)
2. del Galdo, E., Nielsen, J.: International User Interfaces. Wiley, New York (1996)
3. Herskovits, M.: El hombre y sus obras: La ciencia de la antropología cultural. Fondo de Cultura Económica, Mexico (1982)

4. Fischer, G.: Understanding, Fostering, and Supporting Cultures of Participation. Interactions 18(3), 42–53 (2011)
5. Sebeok, T.: Global Semiotics. Indiana University Press, Bloomington (2001)
6. Guha, M., et al.: Working with Young Children as Technology Design Partners. Communications of ACM 48(1), 39–42 (2005)
7. Cipolla-Ficarra, F.: Advances in New Technologies, Interactive Interfaces, and Communicability, pp. 1–7. Springer, Berlin (2010)
8. Multimedia, B.B.C.: CD-ROM Pingu y sus amigos. ZetaMultimedia, Barcelona (1999)
9. Cipolla-Ficarra, F.: Communicability Design and Evaluation in Cultural and Ecological Multimedia Systems. In: Proc. MSCommunicability 2008, pp. 1–8. ACM Press, New York (2008)
10. Wood, L., Skrebowski, L.: The Future's Here; It's Just Unevenly Distributed. Interactions 11(2), 76–79 (2004)
11. Reeves, B., Nass, C.: The Media Equation: How People Treat Computers, Television, and New Media Like Real People and Places. Cambridge University Press, Cambridge (1998)
12. Garrand, T.: Writing for Multimedia. Focal Press, Boston (1997)
13. Thompson, W., et al.: Visual Perception from a Computer Graphics Perspective. CRC Press, New York (2011)
14. Turk, M., Robertson, G.: Perceptual User Interfaces. Communications of the ACM 43(3), 32–34 (2000)
15. Cipolla-Ficarra, F., et al.: Advances in Dynamic and Static Media for Interactive Systems: Communicability, Computer Science and Design. Blue Herons, Bergamo (2011)
16. Silver, H.: Robert Owen on Education. Cambridge University Press, Cambridge (2010)
17. Cipolla-Ficarra, F.V., Cipolla-Ficarra, M., Ficarra, V.M.: Copyright for Interactive Systems: Stratagems for Tourism and Cultural Heritage Promotion. In: Cipolla Ficarra, F.V., de Castro Lozano, C., Nicol, E., Kratky, A., Cipolla-Ficarra, M. (eds.) HCITOCH 2010. LNCS, vol. 6529, pp. 136–147. Springer, Heidelberg (2011)
18. Maestri, G.: Digital Character Animation 3. New Riders Press, Berkeley (2006)
19. Osipa, J.: Stop Staring: Facial Modeling and Animation Done Right. Wiley, New York (2010)
20. Trowbridge, S., Stapleton, C.: Melting the Boundaries Between Fantasy and Reality. IEEE Computer 42(7), 57–62 (2009)

A Security Model for Functional Active Objects

Florian Kammueller

Middlesex University London, U.K.
f.kammueller@mdx.ac.uk

Abstract. In this paper we describe a language based security model for distributed computing based on functional active objects intended to build a basis for Distributed Information Flow Control (DIFC) and contrast it to earlier models in particular the prominent model by Myers and Liskov. We carefully motivate the assumptions concerning secure communication in distributed object-oriented scenarios, show that they naturally lead to futures as the security abstraction of object oriented message passing, and motivate our assumptions by an example. Finally, the stepping stones to a formal foundation of the model are summarized: the notion of visibility, the security classes, and a definition of information-flow security for distributed active objects.

Keywords: Distributed Systems, Security, Functional Active Objects.

1   Introduction

A simple retrospective view into security history shows that classical security models have problems with distributed communicating systems. The high-watermark principle [Wei69] was a security model prior to the Bell-La Padula and MLS security systems [De76]. In this system, objects would just be assigned higher security classes whenever a subject of a higher level interacted with them. Eventually, as a consequence of the above explained crux, the two entities ended up on the same level. The problem that has been encountered here is that entities eventually all swim up and the system as a whole becomes unusable for anyone of lower security classes. The problem could not be resolved in Bell LaPadula or any other Multi-Level Security (MLS) model either, since it is inherent in communication combined with hierarchical security classes where information may only flow up: any remote computation will always consist of a request and a reply. To request something we need to write, so the object that requests must be in a lower or equal security class than the object it requests from (no-write-down). The corresponding reply will also need to write. But the second write is now in the inverse direction, hence the replying object must be lower or equal than the requesting. As a result of this catch-22 situation [Hel56][1], both, requesting and replying objects must be in the same security class which is a trivial scenario rendering the hierarchy idea useless. Unfortunately, this catch also

---

[1] Joseph Heller's famous WWII novel coined this phrase for situations where mutual dependency causes paradoxical situations.

F.V. Cipolla-Ficarra et al. (Eds.): CCGIDIS 2011, LNCS 7545, pp. 42–50, 2012.

applies to distributed systems: any hierarchy, even a trivial one, e.g. public and private, creates it.

In this paper we advocate the use of *futures* as a distributed communication model for object-oriented systems to overcome the catch-22. A future is a promise to the reply of a method call enabling asynchronous computation. However, a future also binds request and reply into one unit and therefore builds the natural abstraction of method passing in catch-22 situations.

Based on this abstraction, we present a new approach to a security model for distributed systems that is a simplification of the widely adopted model for Distributed Information Flow Control (DIFC) [ML97]. The DIFC has recently become very popular again e.g. [HSR10], because distributed software applications and networks grow together. However, researchers usually apply Myers' original security model unchanged to implement information flow control on networked systems although many questions remain unanswered by it. For example, how can we guarantee that adversaries in remote sites respect the DIFC policy?

The simplification we propose is inspired by the concept of RESTful web-services [Fie00] allowing an abstraction to stateless actor-based services. We can thus use the calculus of functional distributed objects ASP_{fun} [HKL11] as a formal basis for the model. The contribution of this paper is a formal model for distributed security for functional active objects. After exploring some situations that explain implicit flows in distributed scenarios (Section 2), we introduce the new security model abstractly by defining visibility and security classification (Section 3). We finally compare and contrast our approach to other major approaches and give a short outlook (Section 5).

The model presented in this paper augments the formal definition of noninterference presented in an earlier paper [Kam11].

2   Information Flow Control for Functional Active Objects

Language based security uses separation of concern to master security issues. In the following we characterize our view on this discipline elaborating the security assumptions made. One important design principle for the design of secure systems is the establishment of a security perimeter [Gol08]. The security design is then centered on the question on how we can prevent an attacker from getting access to a layer below our protection mechanism. If we assume the security perimeter to be an operating system that supports a security-enhanced language, we can assume that the attacker is bound to the means provided by this language. In other words, the attacker cannot get to the layer below the language. For example, he cannot compromise the run-time system and gaining information can only be performed using methods provided by the language. This is the assumption that is taken in language-based security - although it is usually not spelled out very clearly since it is a seemingly strong assumption. However, without this assumption we cannot hope to define a decent protection mechanism. In particular considering the above explained catch-22, even within this security perimeter given by language based security, it is still questionable whether we can arrive at a useful model for security of distributed systems.

Our model is a simplified DIFC model[2]. We take the view of a multilateral security world, in which there is not one hierarchical security hierarchy as in the classical Bell-LaPadula or multi-level security (MLS) models [De76] but instead all principals have their private space that is not accessible by anyone; all principals have, however, access to a common public domain. The situation is most simply expressed graphically as in Figure 1.

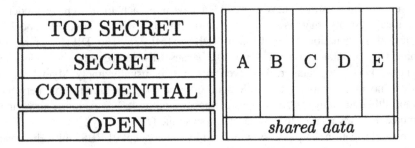

Fig. 1. Multi-level security versus multilateral security [Ch. 8, And01]

More concretely, we model distributed systems as a set of actors that have unique identities and possess a set of public methods providing services to other actors.

Simultaneously, these actors may have a private part constituted again by methods that may only be used by themselves. Keeping with the philosophy of RESTful systems, we consider network based distributed systems as stateless [Ch. 5.1.3, Fie00]. That is, in the abstraction we use for our model we use no mutable state for our actors.

Actors may nevertheless change according to method or attribute updates; however, we consider those actors to be different from their original thereby modelling evolution as a series of actor instances. The stateless view enables the treatment of communications in a functional object-oriented style. The public area depicted on the bottom in Figure 1 on the right side is constituted in our model by the public methods of all actors within range.

This first part of our distributed security model is a RESTful actor (or object) model.

For the second part, the communication model, we adopt also an object-oriented view but one fitting in naturally with distributed functional actors: *futures* [Hal85]. A future is a simple way of representing remote method invocation (and similar communication concepts) by unifying call and reply in one identifiable unit: the future. By definition, a future is a promise to the reply of a method call. We consider the future as the ideal security abstraction for request and reply of object-oriented message passing because of the catch-22 paradox. Since we cannot avoid the catch-22, we may as well abstract any bilateral communication by one atomic abstraction unit: the future.

---

[2] For an in depth comparison of the new proposition to the classical model see Section 5.

These two ingredients, distributed objects (or actors) and future based communication form a viable basis for modelling distributed systems. However, to model confidentiality we need to specify visibility. For our model we make the following two assumptions:

[LB] the computation of method calls inside actors is only accessible by the future representing that call, i.e. it is only visible to the invoker of this call (or anyone that has received the future from this invoker).

[VI] Actors α are identified uniquely by a name α and are visible to any other actor β knowing that name; actor β can only access (invoke) the *public* methods of α.

Note, that in assumption **[VI]** β's access to a public method invocation, for example $\alpha.m$, in α is exclusive to β: due to assumption **[LB]**, α has no access to $\alpha.m$. This may seem to be a strong assumption but it is a natural consequence of the language based security approach combined with the adoption of the functional RESTful language model.

We next give a motivating example that illustrates the view of actors and at the same time shows the implicit flows that may lead to illicit gain of information from an attackers viewpoint.

3   Service Example with Security Critical Information Flow

We present the example using the calculus of functional active objects \aspfun [HKL11]. The language is a computation model for functional active objects; an implementation called Erlang active objects is available [FK10]. ASP$_{fun}$ represents the current global state as a configuration of activities. The activities have a name and a request list containing all the requests that have been demanded to this activity. In Figure 2, we see the three activities α, client, and broker of our service example. The client can book via the broker a hotel room the choice of which depends on the purse: if there are less than 50 euros, only the cheap room, otherwise the luxury room. The privacy issue is that the client's name and purse contents remain confidential. On the request queue of the client we already see a request to the method bookcheap of the broker as result of a prior call to book.

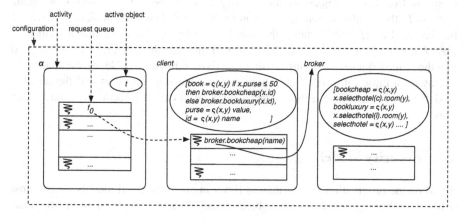

Fig. 2. ASP$_{fun}$: service example

Each activity has its request queue, formally a set that contains so-called *futures*:

For example in Figure 2, f_0 is a future defined in client as a result of a previous call from α to the book method of client. The future f_0 is used in α's request list. This reference is represented as a dashed arrow in the figure. The solid arrow, by contrast, is an activity reference to broker used in the future f_0. The example configuration of Figure 2 is syntactically expressed as follows.

$$\alpha[f_\alpha \to f_0, t]$$
$$\| \text{ client}[f_0 \mapsto \text{broker.bookcheap(name)},$$
$$[\text{book} = \varsigma(x, y)\text{if } x.\text{purse} \leq 50$$
$$\qquad \text{then broker.bookcheap}(x.\text{id}) \text{ else broker.bookluxury}(x.\text{id}),$$
$$\text{purse} = \varsigma(x, y)\text{value},$$
$$\text{id} = \varsigma(x, y)\text{name}]$$
$$\| \text{ broker}[\varnothing, [\text{bookcheap} = \varsigma(x, y)x.\text{selecthotel}(c).\text{room}(y),$$
$$\text{bookluxury} = \varsigma(x, y)x.\text{selecthotel}(l).room(y),$$
$$\text{selecthotel} = \varsigma(x, y) \dots]]$$

An implicit information flow can be contained not only inside a program evaluation, like in the example given in the introduction, where the statements c and d in the branches of an if convey information about the guard. Exactly the same information loss can flow on depending on the effects the statements c and d have. In our running example, the decision taken in the client to call bookcheap instead of bookluxury conveys the information that the client's purse is <= 50. This information is then carried over in the call to broker and may be visible in the instantiation of the selecthotel method. We did not include any detail about the selecthotel implementation but, say, that selecthotel(c) creates a call to ibis.room whereas selecthotel(l) creates a call to hilton.room instead. Thus, there is an implicit flow from client.purse via bookcheap to ibis.room. Given that broker is considered as a non-trustworthy object, we must therefore demand that the entry in the request list of the broker is invisible to hostile parts and even to the broker. More generally, if we represent trustworthy objects by the security class H and non-trustworthy or public ones by L, the results of both methods in broker bookcheap and bookluxury have to be classified as H. Furthermore, the attacker model must assume that activities of class L may still contain methods that return H and that these returns that are queued into the request queue of the surrounding L-activity remain invisible for the attacker.

Based on these informal observations on possible implicit flows and the attacker model, we will next give a more formal security model that allows to control such flows.

4   Security Model

Based on the observation of information flows in object-oriented models we can now define visibility in a function active object model. Visibility is the pillar on which our security model is based.

4.1   Visibility and Security Classes

Visibility is defined recursively over references in methods: a method containing references to a set of activities sees all methods of these activities and (recursively) everything in the range of visibility of these methods. The base case is a method with no references whose visibility range is given by this method. The visibility range of an activity is given by the union of the visibility ranges of its methods. A formal definition of visibility range in ASP_{fun} is straightforward but beyond the scope of this paper.

Given the visibility through possible information flows in an object-oriented model, we can now integrate security classes to be assigned to the actors, their methods and data (attributes)[3].

The security classification is on two levels, internal and global. The classification is a direct consequence of the multilateral view of the world.

Global Classification. The global security classification is based on the classical structure of a security lattice [De76] composed of the (private/public)-level and the canonical complete lattice over the identities of the active objects. More precisely, this lattice **L** is given as

$$\langle (\{L, H\} \times \mathcal{P}(\mathcal{I}), \sqsubseteq)$$

where I is the set of all identities of active objects, and the ordering is defined as

$$(L_0, I_0) \sqsubseteq (L_1, I_1) \equiv \left(\begin{array}{c} L_0 <_L L_1 \vee L_0 = L_1 \\ I_0 \subseteq I_1 \end{array} \right)$$

with

$$<_L = \{(L, H)\}$$

the ordering on the security levels. The lattice **L** is a complete lattice because

- the join of two elements $(L_0, I_0), (L_1, I_1)$ is $(max(L_0, L_1), I_0 \cup I_1)$,
- the meet of two elements $(L_0, I_0), (L_1, I_1)$ is $(min(L_0, L_1), I_0 \cap I_1)$,
- there is a bottom element $(L, \varnothing)$,
- and there is a top element (H, I).

The global classification is a direct consequence of the local classification and the visibility: any active object α visible to β must be dominated by it. Hence, if β is visible by α, α's class is above β's. That is, for an activity α, its security class is $C_\alpha \cup$ "the security classes of all activities in α's visibility range".

---

[3] Methods and attributes are viewed uniformly which is natural in an object oriented world since an object's attribute is one-to-one represented by the method that returns its value.

4.2   Application to Running Example

As a simple illustration of the security model consider the running example from Section 3. There, we already sketched the danger of illicit information flows given a simple high-low partition of the world. What we want to show now is that the refined security model given in the previous section enables a fine-grained specification of the information flow control.

Let us first determine the visibility ranges of the application in particular of the possible attacker α. In its request queue he has a future f_0 that must have been created by a call to one of α's methods, say $\alpha.m$ in t. This method m must read $\varsigma\ (x,y)$ client.book(client.name). Therefore, α's visibility range contains the method client.book and α's method m dominates client's methods book and name.

Although the method purse is not in the visibility range of α, it can learn (at least some information about) the value of purse by the result of book: an illicit information flow.

We can use the security classification to statically detect this illicit flow. Since the secret value purse is a confidential value of client, in the internal security specification of client the method purse must be classified as H. A local information flow analysis immediately shows that the method book depends on the value of purse. This can be statically detected because the self x is used inside the definition of book and its high component purse is invoked. In a practical implementation a simple type checking can purely locally to client decide this violation of the security policy.

5   Conclusions

Andrew C. Myers developed in his PhD with Barbara Liskow one of the most successful security models for distributed applications: distributed information flow control (DIFC) or later named, the decentralized label model (DLM) [ML97].

Myers also pioneered practical implementations of this model by the Jif tool [Mye99], an information flow package for Java. The Jif methodology only applies if the Jif library based on Java is globally used, including the enforcement of Jif-signatures on all Java classes from the very foundation upwards. In current research activities, e.g. [HSR10], we see a revival of the DIFC idea by reimplementing the original model directly in operating systems.

Myers DIFC uses two abstractions *slots* (variables, objects, and other storage locations) and *values* (defined indirectly by ``computations manipulate values'' [ML97]). Slots serve as sources and sinks for values but values can also be obtained from *input channels* - which are read only slots for entering information to the system. In Myers model, an *owner* of an object can downgrade the label of a value. This procedure is called *relabeling* (although in reality it is the copy of a value which gets a new label). To ensure that an information flow is secure - in brief - it is sufficient to check that the relabeling is consistent with the security policy. *Only values can be relabeled - slots and channels cannot.*

These basic abstractions already show the difference from our security model: Myers model is decisively static and imperative. We use a functional model and dynamic creation of new activities is naturally coped with in our model. On the other hand, Myers advocates declassification of values as a decisive feature of DIFC. The declassification is indeed an important feature for hierarchical security models where a security level can swim up (remember the high watermark principle).

We completely leave out declassification in our model but security classification is mandatory (i.e. fixed) in our model. On one side, this seems to be a restriction but on the other side it helps to statically decide security classification enabling implementation of compile time security type checking. What is more, this restriction is based on the observation that catch-22 is inevitable and may as well be abstracted by the future.

In some sense, futures correspond to communication channels similar to those used in the DIFC model and also other more conservative models of distributed security, e.g. [SM02]. This analogy also shows the decisive difference of futures: channels are not dynamic whereas a future is dynamically created with every single method call.

The security model presented in this paper is the building block for constructing analysis methods for functional active objects. As illustrated in the small example in this paper, a given security assignment on a distributed active object system may be given but is not necessarily secure: implicit flows may exist because local security assignments do not take into account the visibility and the resulting global security classifications. Illicit information flows occur. The whole point of a security model it to use the foundation to devise efficient techniques to detect and avoid such application scenarios. As a next step, we plan to define a security type system for the ASP_{fun} language to show that it is possible to automatically check for such flaws in a given security assignment.

References

[And01] Anderson, R.: Security Engineering – A Guide to Building Dependable Distributed Systems. Wiley (2001)

[Den76] Denning, D.E.: Lattice model of secure information flow. Communications of the ACM 19(5), 236–242 (1976)

[Fie00] Fielding, R.T.: Architectural Styles and the Design of Network-based Software Architectures. PhD thesis, University of California, Irvine (2000)

[FK10] Fleck, A., Kammüller, F.: Implementing privacy with erlang active objects. In: 5th International Conference on Internet Monitoring and Protection, ICIMP 2010. IEEE (2010)

[Gol08] Gollmann, D.: Computer Security. McGraw-Hill (2008)

[Hal85] Halstead Jr., R.H.: Multilisp: A language for concurrent symbolic computation. ACM Transactions on Programming Languages and Systems (TOPLAS) 7(4), 501–538 (1985)

[Hel61] Heller, J.: Catch-22. Vintage (1994), 1961

[HJR10] Harris, W.R., Jha, S., Reps, T.: Difc programs by automatic instrumentation. In: Proceedings of the 17th ACM Conference on Computer and Communications Security, CCS 2010, pp. 284–296. ACM, New York (2010)

[HKL11] Henrio, L., Kammüller, F., Lutz, B.: Aspfun: A typed functional active object calculus. Science of Computer Programming (2011) (in print)

[Kam11] Kammüller, F.: Privacy Enforcement and Analysis for Functional Active Objects. In: Garcia-Alfaro, J., Navarro-Arribas, G., Cavalli, A., Leneutre, J. (eds.) DPM 2010 and SETOP 2010. LNCS, vol. 6514, pp. 93–107. Springer, Heidelberg (2011)

[ML97] Myers, A.C., Liskov, B.: A decentralized model for information flow control. In: Proceedings of the Sixteenth ACM Symposium on Operating Systems Principles, SOSP 1997, pp. 129–142. ACM, New York (1997)

[Mye99] Myers, A.C.: Jflow: Practical mostly-static information flow control. In: 26th ACM Symposium on Principles of Programming Languages, POPL 1999 (1999)

[SM02] Sabelfeld, A., Mantel, H.: Securing Communication in a Concurrent Language. In: Hermenegildo, M.V., Puebla, G. (eds.) SAS 2002. LNCS, vol. 2477, pp. 376–394. Springer, Heidelberg (2002)

[Wei69] Weissmann, C.: Security controls in the ADEPT-50 timesharing system. In: AFIPS Conference, pp. 119–133. FJCC (1969)

Ergonomy, Industrial Design and Divine Proportion

Francisco V. Cipolla Ficarra[1,2]

HCI Lab. – F&F Multimedia Communications Corp.
[1] ALAIPO: Asociación Latina de Interacción Persona-Ordenador
[2] AINCI: Asociación Internacional de la Comunicación Interactiva
c/ Angel Baixeras, 5 – AP 1638, 08080 Barcelona, Spain
Via Pascoli, S. 15 – CP 7, 24121 Bergamo, Italy
ficarra@alaipo.com

Abstract. In the current work is stressed the importance of the classical notions of design in mobile computing. With this purpose is analyzed the bidirectional relationship between divine proportion, ergonomy and industrial design. Besides, the main reasons are presented why it is necessary to count on a communicability expert in order to get high quality products and services with low costs. The importance of visualization of graphic computing in the era of the expansion of communicability with small-size interactive screens is also made apparent. Finally, the results of heuristic assessment carried out with adult and inexperienced users in the use of interactive systems belonging to the mobile computing set are presented.

Keywords: Ergonomy, Industrial Design, Divine Proportion, Interactive Systems, Interfaces, Heuristic Evaluation.

1   Introduction

Since remote times, the human being has developed numerical systems to carry out his main activities. Each ancient civilization has depicted them in its own way, but since the origins of these numerical systems the human being has used them to count, rank, measure and codify. Among these four activities the former two go back to the earliest cultures in the history of civilization. Whereas the latter two make up a subset of more recent activities in this evolution process. Now one of the key elements of the 20th century has been the need to carry out great calculations in the shortest possible time [1] [2] [3]. That is, that to these operations was added the time variable, because the shorter the time to solve complex problems, the greater the benefits for the evolution of the production industries and services institutions. It was so that many employees started to use the calculators with their basic functions, until they were divided into scientific, graphic and programmable, for instance. We find in them the first antecedents of mobile computing. Simultaneously were developed other subsets, such as : information appliances (personal digital assistants, pocket computers, mobile phones, e-books, handheld game consoles, etc.), laptops (subnotebooks, desktop replacement computers, etc.), tablet computers (tablet PCs, ultra-mobile PCs, mobile Internet devices, etc.), laptops (netbooks, smartbooks, etc.), and wearable computers

F.V. Cipolla-Ficarra et al. (Eds.): CCGIDIS 2011, LNCS 7545, pp. 51–66, 2012.

(melme-mounted displays, calculator watch). Devices which could be held in both hands, one hand, leaning or not on a flat surface, but which in the micro range also start from the calculator, as in the case of the calculator wrist watch. Now the ergonomy for each one of these small-size devices required important financial resources for the analysis, in the prototype development stage. The ergonomy that the interaction with these devices allows together with communicability are key factors in the continuous evolution of mobile computing.

The word ergonomics appeared published in a newspaper article written by Wojciech Jastrzebowski, in 1857, defining it as the science of work. Some words associated with ergonomics from the point of view of computer science are: communicability, comfort, usability, etc. It is a notion that has set the path to be followed so that the human being can be involved in the working environment in the most natural way [4]. Etymologically, the term "ergonomics" (from the Greek –ergon (work) and nomos (rules) was implemented little by little in the academic environment. The first to talk about industrial ergonomics was the Englishman Murrell in the late 1940s [4]. That is, a scientific area where several disciplines interact, which would need computer simulations to reach that wellbeing goal for people in their working environment, for instance. Two decades later, in 1961, the International Association of Ergonomics was born (www.sea.cc).

In the relationship of the human being with the environment, perhaps a small afterthought can be made from the point of view of science philosophy, resorting to the classical notions of Mario Bunge [5], from Tomás Maldonado's industrial design [6]. However, a fast way to focus the issue is Murrell's definition, who claims that "ergonomics consists in adapting work to man" [7], thus inverting the premise sustained by Taylor and Ford in the last century, when they referred to the theory of industrial organization and machines. These two authors contended that man had to be adapted to work [7]. Evidently, some totally obsolete concepts in front of the notion of the global village, suggested by McLuhan and the democratization of the access to digital information through the Internet starting from the mid 90s [8]. Exceptionally, this theory was in force in the industrial sector of the components companies in the new millennium, especially in the 2D and/or 3D design. Virtual companies that put at the disposal of off-line and on-line multimedia materials millions of pieces related to mechanics, electronics, etc. which made up a great digital free library for graphic designers but which the company leaders anchored in obsolete models of the working system banned the access to the Internet of the designers in the centre of Europe [9]. As a rule, when in the centennial industrial sector technological progress is stopped, ergonomy together with research and development are absent. A communicability expert can detect the degree of openness to technological innovation of a centennial company starting from the analysis of the content of the websites and the company image they want to sell [10]. The readers interested in these issues can delve deeper into this subject in the following bibliography [11] [12].

2   Interfaces and Interaction

For decades understanding the physical aspect of the stable components of an interface in a computer has turned out to be more simple than analyzing the variable components of the people who interact with the computer through the interface. The set of users from the point of view of design has always been divided according to age, the computer knowledge, the motivation of the interaction, etc. Factors that must be taken into account at the moment of creating products and services through the interactive systems, trying to encompass the greatest possible number of users, with or without physical disabilities. When the metaphor of an interface is designed, it is done in such a way that the communicability is present to make easier the tasks it carries out, always trying to gain in productivity and personal satisfaction. Now when real objects are planned with which we interact physically, for instance, mice, keyboards, etc., they follow a set of rules which make up a guideline to be followed in a lineal way [13]. In regard to the size, the ability of the body, the human senses are well catalogued and described inside ergonomics.

Fig. 1. The multimedia system presents an excellent combination of the dynamic and static media that existed at the time

In some occasions inside human-computer interaction we find ergonomics linked to health, software and technology, cognitive psychology and the social aspects. With graphic software any object can be designed or planned to solve current problems or open new ways through the inventions, knowing beforehand that it will have a good functionality, although the real prototypes haven't been made. Such a statement is due to the fact that a good designer, for instance, would not design a control board where a user must actuate simultaneously two levers which are at 5 meters distance. As a rule, there is a tendency to design for the highest possible percentage of the population. Something similar happens with the interfaces. Now this notion of percentages is in direct relationship to ergonomics. The ideal thing is always to reach the 100% of the population, that is, the potential users.

These days, adapting the work to people guarantees the maximal convenience and safety of all those devoted to design since the start. Evidently, it is a principle that many graphic software manufacturers to discern, who have firmly bet on the democratization of bidimensional and three-dimensional images, whether they are static or dynamic, since 1990 for the users of personal computers, for instance.

Others, in contrast, have plumped for the high range of the hardware such as the workstation. Now, aside from the software and the hardware, the good industrial designer must always respond to three rhetoric questions since the very origin of the project:

- Who will use the product? That is, the traditional analysis of the potential users from a perspective of several converging disciplines. This is what many currently call "user-focused design" but which has its roots in ergonomics for many decades.
- What thing will be used? That is, the object must be analyzed from the perspective of formal and informal use, to the intrinsic characteristics that define it and communicate its use, starting from the information brochures down to the training to use it correctly.
- Where will it be used? The context where it will be inserted both from a physical and a sociocultural perspective.

The computer-made images generally still have their origin in a simple sheet of paper and exceptionally in the computer, through programs for vector images or bitmap. Once the first ideas have been represented they can be taken to a program for 3D modelling. Since 1980, the compatibility of the files tends to be universal, especially with the graphics of office automation (representation of the losses and the profits of a commercial activity, the industrial production times comparing two different methods and/or techniques, etc.) tends to be of 100%.

This compatibility was guaranteed as being synonymous with quality in the last century, since there was work underway in 2D and/or 3D design including self-editing or digital photography. An example in this regard are the Autodesk products and especially 3D Studio, which along time will change their name in relation to the evolution of the operative systems of the PCs [14]. In the latest versions of 3D Max for the Windows Vista and XP Professional operative systems (32 bits version and 64 bits, respectively), the use of a material editor for nodes is allowed (i.e., www.node.joe.com), what means a saving of time at the moment of making the first tests of the objects that make up the scene. In this regard, the software "Schematic Material Editor" made by Jerry Vlilammi and distributed as Software Open Source (i.e., http://www.ylilammi.com/tools.shtml) also deserves some mention. The advantage of these tools is the possibility of rapidly finding out the components of the materials in the shape of a tree, considerably reducing the production costs of the first prototypes of the product that is being designed.

Responding to the three rhetorical questions of ergonomics, many graphical software commercial products with international distribution have been an important means of work to carry out the first computer tests, introducing changes in an agile and simple way in 2D and/or 3D design. A study along time allows us to know that many professionals of the graphic arts (analogical) who started to use the computers and the commercial software to generate images in vector and/or bitmap sector, currently are real experts in static and dynamic images for mobile computing. It was they who transferred the wealth of experiences and theoretical knowledge related to cognitive psychology, fine arts, semiotics, etc. to the digital context, since the first off-line multimedia systems.

Fig. 2. The democratization of the 2D and the 3D design has boosted an avant-garde design where the only limit is creativity

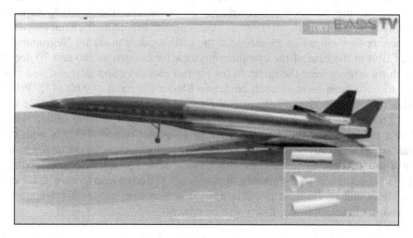

Fig. 3. The computer animation in the Web 2.0 (http://www.eads.com/eads/int/en/eadstv.html) consents to shape an image of objects with an innovative design for next decades

Many of those interactive systems are excellent examples even today. This is due to the fact that these contents are complete synthesis in the interrelations between the formal and the factual sciences in spite of the storage limitations in the CD-Rom [13], the DVD or Web 2.0. Some good examples can be found in the figures 1, 2, and 3 on the design of ergonomic products of the past, present and future:

In the figure 3 it can be seen one of the main applications of graphic computing which is the simulation of the future through the means of public transportation, in this case the project of the Zehst (Zero Emission Hyper Sonic Transport) plane, which theoretically in 2050 will cover the Paris-Tokyo route in 90 minutes. The goal of these 3D representations is not only to create an imaginary collective of the future societies and obtain adherents or financial partners for the project.

The avant-garde design does not only allow us to imagine new conditions of the daily life of the inhabitants, but very often the objects or products that make up that imaginary reality may be anticipated in time. The invention of new functions of the existing ones or the new problems posed to the existing ones is the starting point. In this sense, it is enough to analyze the evolution in time of the phone and the computer, since the moment in which a first convergence has taken place. These convergences are sources of production of goods and services which have their origin in industrial design, for instance.

3   Cognitive Psychology, Divine Proportion and Communicability: Intersection

Together with industrial design an endless series of products has been designed for the physical interaction with computers where all the limitations of the potential users have been examined and classified. Excepting the keyboard which has followed the disposition of the traditional typewriters, the mice and the joystick have been constantly modified until arriving at the current ergonomic characteristics. A diachronic review allows us to see since the early models made by Negroponte and Richard Bolt in the case of the computer joystick for computers (60 and 70 decades) although its origins were the controls for aircraft elevators and ailerons, and is first known to have been used as such on Louis Bleriot's aircraft (1908) [15]. Whereas Douglas Engelbart, with the help of Bill English elaborate the first prototype of the mouse. The first known publication of the term "mouse" as a pointing device is in Bill English's 1965 publication "Computer-Aided Display Control" [15]. In both cases, we can see how an invention must be adapted to the human characteristics of the potential users. These days, we constantly have to design products for intellectual and less physical activities. Consequently, if one wants to design interfaces which work in the best way and in the least possible time, it is necessary to develop some mental ergonomics, where communicability will be present.

3.1   Visualization of the Information and Cognitive Psychology

The study of the operative environment of the mental abilities of the users is cognitive psychology. This discipline has as a goal of study the basic and deep mechanisms through which knowledge is elaborated, from perception, memory and learning, down to the formation of concepts and logical reasoning. However, there are some who call it cognitive engineering in the context of systems engineering [16]. However, putting the word engineering to an existing discipline and deriving from the social sciences may entail the redundancy, ambiguity and loss of relationship between signification and signifier in the classical notion of sign presented by Saussure. In this sense, it is necessary to make clear that cognitive systems engineering is a branch of systems engineering which deals with the cognitive bodies, whether they are human or not, like a type of systems capable of dealing with information and using cognitive resources such as perception, memory or the information processing. It depends on the direct application of experience and research both in cognitive psychology as in systems engineering.

Evidently, inside the communicative process and in a special way in communicability we must take into account that the user in front of a computer screen, for instance, is facing texts, graphics, pictures, etc. starting from the learning process of some rudiments of cognitive psychology, which studies the interrelation between perception, memory and knowledge. From that point of view there are interesting studies of the static image and those stemming from mathematics and geometry [17] [18] [19]. Computer graphics had a great field of expansion in the office automation of the 80s, especially with the statistics since the statistic graphics work so well to communicate certain kinds of information. In the case of the interface designer, he/she must possess at least theoretical notions of how perception works, memory and reasoning mechanisms. In some way his/her final products must always have as a goal helping in this process. Obviously, if he or she follows this path they are implicitly and explicitly helping communicability.

Perception, the processing of information deriving from the senses, understanding and memory have many limitations and particularities. Understanding them in depth is a must to be a good communicator, to present graphics effectively. Being capable of foreseeing how the potential users will process some content helps not to be a prey to the weaknesses of the mind and profit at the same time from its inborn skills. Now this information does not only apply to static graphics, but also to the texts. In this sense, and for reasons of commercial costs of the telecommunications in Southern Europe [15], the written word generally prevails over the verbal word, through audiovisual mobile phones, for instance. Besides, with mobile phones (SMS –Short Message Service) and the emails, the human being has exponentially multiplied the hours they write with the keyboard in relation to the 70s, in which in the offices were used the classical typewriters of the early 20th century. If we analyze the evolution of the hypermedia, with the hypertext it was already necessary to follow certain rules in the making of the messages due to the limitations of the hardware and/or software for the telecommunications at that time. However, for a good communicability expert it is essential to know the way to write the texts as well as the graphics beforehand. There is no difference at all between both (image and static text) in the sense that learning how the eyes and the brain work is an advantage to any professional. The only way to acquire this knowledge is through a solid college training, where the formal and the factual sciences converge.

The visualization of information is an area in constant growth, and in a special way in the time of communicability expansion. According to the most usual definition in Stephen's foundational texts, it is a discipline that has as its goal to create interactive graphic presentations which "widen cognition", the perceptive and understanding abilities [17]. Evidently, it is necessary to carry out always a distinction between depictive graphics and symbolic graphics [17]. A depictive graphic is that which has a resemblance with what it depicts, like the map of a city, the explanations of the components of a classical painting, the elements that make a clock work mechanically, etc. In a symbolic graphic, on the contrary, the relationship with the depicted phenomenon is formal, as in the case of the statistic graphics. Now the way of reading and interpreting these two types of graphic depends on every person. The reading of the former is simple but in order to understand the latter one has got to learn certain conventions: that there are axes X and Y (here is important the notion of the divine proportion, for instance) that the height of the bars is proportional to the amounts they codify, etc. Currently the statistic graphics are very common, so that we think that their reading is natural, but it isn't. In this regard the conclusions reached by Mitroff are interesting [17]. She has demonstrated that not everybody understands graphics of statistics easily. Everything depends on the activation patterns of certain brain regions which vary depending on the individual. Mitroff [17] showed that architects, engineers, artists and scientists interpret graphics in different ways. The same happens with the common readers and the computer users who are not experts in computer science.

A designer of interactive systems who intends to generate contents for computer screens must follow two main principles which boost the communicability of the content: the relevance and the right knowledge. The principle of "relevance", which means that a graphic must contain only the amount of information necessary to sustain an argumentation, or tell a story in the case of the video or the computer animations. In fact, the principle is applicable both to graphics and to texts: before starting to work, one must consider what one wants to say.

The second, the principle of "right knowledge" establishes that we must use codes that our potential users understand beforehand. That is, the quality attributes that we call transparency of meaning, for instance [15]. It is acceptable to use innovating graphics, but always being mindful of including clues and explanations so that the reader doesn't get lost. Something similar happens to the text: we do not write in the same way for expert or specialized users as for a rookie user of an interactive system. The designer of the interactive systems makes decisions on what should be included or not, and on how to do it. So that both principles are applicable, the designer must have an idea of the kind of questions that the users will want to have answered, and choose the data and program the interface according to them. In any case, we guess that those graphics are so overwhelming that most users do not pay attention to them.

3.2 Divine Proportion and Golden Ratio

In the first off-line multimedia systems (i.e., Art Gallery [20], Le Louvre [21], Renoir [22]), whose contents refer to the cultural heritage, we find 2D animations to explain some of the phenomena that at first sight an observer of a painting, for instance, contemporaneous or not, would overlook. These issues refer to mathematics and geometry, which also exist in the current interfaces of the mobile computing: multimedia phones, Tablet PCs, etc. and which are grouped under the name of "golden ratio", divine proportion or golden number. It is a figure which is known since Antiquity and it appears in a repetitive way in the artistic, architectural constructions, etc., resulting from the following equation:

$$\frac{1+\sqrt{5}}{2} \cong 1.6180339887$$

Now by applying this number to one of the sides of a rectangle results in a golden rectangle, that is, a geometric figure which has lasted along the evolution of computer monitors since cathode rays tubes until liquid crystal screens, including the current mini-screens of microcomputing.

If we analyze the screens of the television sets that were plugged to the earliest Commodore computers, for instance, which allowed one to program in BASIC and interact with the first videogames, they belonged to the set of the classical size of the television sets in the 4-3 proportion. In the flat and digital television sets the proportion is 16-9. In both cases it is the ratio of the length of their sides. If one watches a film on both screens the huge effect can be seen of the proportion of the frame on the image that it contains. In the television sets of the 80s, for instance, the human figures are longer (vertical) and on the flat screens they are more stunted (horizontal). The problem is that they are not rectangles of the same shape. In other words, the panoramic television sets distort horizontally the sign of the traditional TV because the screen is longer. However, the horizontal disposition for the reading of the texts on the screens has brought about an almost natural process in the users of the computers which in some aspects has slowed down the circulation and expansion of other vertical screens such as the E-books or the early models of the Global Positioning System (GPS). In the late 19th century, Gustav Fechner (pioneer of physical psychology [19]) carried out experiments with inexperienced people of the visual arts so that they chose between several rectangular shapes, including squares, mostly they have chosen those with the dimension of the divine proportion or golden rectangle.

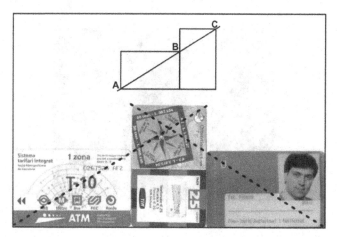

Fig. 4. The point C inside the computer screen is that which most strikes the attention of the user in Western culture

Now placing both rectangles together, one horizontal and another vertical, a diagonal may be drawn from the base of the first until the upper part of the second. If this line touches the three vortexes A, B and C , as can be seen in the figure 4, we can conclude that many objects of daily life (bus tickets, phonecards, old university pass, etc.) have been designed following the principles of the divine proportion in the mind.

Geometric figures which do follow this ratio are usually visually agreeable from the visual point of view. These golden rectangles were used in the works of Leonardo Da Vinci, Georges Seurat, Salvador Dalí, etc. Leonardo Da Vinci and Luca Pacioli (author of the book "De divina proportione" where the proportions that must be kept to achieve beauty starting from geometry are set [19]) were those who introduced that golden number as a sign of beauty inside art. Following these notions of aesthetic and mathematics, in the mid 90s it was possible to design and carry out in a short time the first educational interactive systems for the first virtual university in Barcelona [23]. The results were excellent, especially for those computer and Internet users who were inexperienced, thus allowing several thousands of potential virtual students to acquire university degrees (mainly disciplines of the social sciences) without leaving the home or the office. Consequently, the theory derived from the Italian Renaissance with its main representatives of the sciences (artists, architects, philosophers, mathematicians, among others) have fostered these notions in Western culture. However, inside the context of architecture and the rectangles, we have the Cordobesian "Córdoba rectangle" of octagonal mihrab (Rafael de la Hoz [19]) in the Mosque of Córdoba. The architect de la Hoz framed the proportions that he had gathered as a rectangle whose sides are the radio of the circumference and the side of the regular octagon inscribed on it. The formula that determines the Córdoba proportion or Córdoba number is what follows:

$$\frac{R}{S} = \frac{1}{\sqrt{2-\sqrt{2}}} \cong 1.307$$

The result can be seen in the figure 4, whose aspect is less elongated that the golden rectangle.

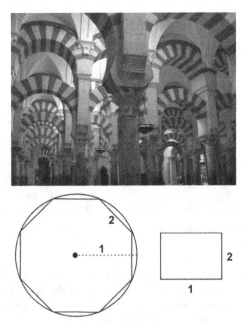

Fig. 5. The cordobesian rectangle in the Mosque of Córdoba

Current experiments with rectangles that emulate the dimension of the new flat television sets, the DIN A folios, etc. are still chosen according to the golden ratio [19]. The influence of the golden ratio and its different manifestations can be seen in classical Greece, but the momentum was with the arts in the Renaissance.

Now the artistic works made since Antiquity in Persia, Egypt, China, etc., had their basis in the observation of nature. It was Leonardo Da Vinci in the Renaissance who unravelled the keys in the flora and fauna, for instance. That is why that they are also in the logarithms spiral present in the shell of a snail, shell of the nautilus, entrepreneurial logos (figure 5) etc. Excluding the text, the entrepreneurial logo is made up in the following way:

Fig. 6. In the succession of quadrants the so-called logarithmic spiral is achieved

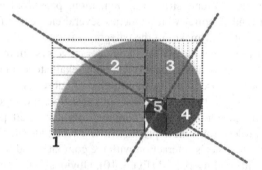

Fig. 7. The diagonals and focal point

If the diagonals are drawn as in the figure 6 where they cross we have a very important focal point for the youngest television viewers or computer users in the Western world. In the 20th century, Cornelius Escher [24] made interesting impossible figures with the spirals, as it can be seen in the following figures:

Fig. 8. In this figure can be seen another of his impossible geometrical three-dimensional frames in the shape of a spiral

Fig. 9. Escher was an artist who didn't know mathematics but had a high level of observation particularly for geometry

The spiral is a curve whose shape does not change when its size is modified, whether it is increased or decreased. This property is called self-similarity. This is a property which can be related to the notion of isotopy in an interface, that is, that set of design elements which are kept constant in the whole interactive system. The design in the on-line and off-line interactive systems is made up by several categories, presentation or layout, content, structure, navigation, panchronism, etc. [15]. The isotopies exist as a kind of spiral which touches several elements of these categories. In short, in the elements that make up the categories is present the notion of beauty, but it is easy and fast to detect the quality of an interactive system in its absence.

The task of the communicability expert who must evaluate an interactive system is to find these isotopies that are to be found as a kind of curves or invisible lines, in the shape of a spiral and which touches elements of the different categories of design of the analyzed system. In contrast, if the communicability expert participates in the final stage of the project for a new product, it must include all the aspects of the disciplines related to the user's interaction with the computer and in which there is an intersection space with said users [25] (figure 10). Obviously, the notions of cognitive psychology and divine proportion will be present in a direct or indirect way.

User Centered Design	Design & Categories	Usability	Design & Emotion	Software & Systems Quality
		communicability		
Human Computer Interaction	Participatory Design	Critical Design	Cognitive Models	Human Factors & Ergonomics

Fig. 10. The localization of communicability

4   Experiments and Results

The experiment was carried out with users inexperienced in the use of computers, whose ages oscillated between 65-75 years of age, of both sexes and without any physical disability. All of them made up a group of 12 users. The techniques used were direct observation and an interview. The experiment took place in a lab of human-computer interaction in Southern Europe and two observers intervened, whose results were merged into a single report and one set of graphics. It began with a test of the shapes of the devices in rectangle shape, following the work by Gustav Fechner for which were simulated the device screens of mobile computing [19] of different brands and models in cardboard and which referred to scientific and graphic calculators, watch calculators, personal digital assistants (PDA), pocket computers, mobile phones, e-books, handheld game consoles, subnotebooks, netbooks and tablet PCs. The participants in the test had to choose only three of these rectangles and order them in relation to their liking of them, following a decreasing order. Later on the participants were invited to carry out four basic operations of addition, subtraction, multiplication and division., using only number two, that is, 2+2, 2-2, 2x2 and 2/2 in the following real devices: a scientific calculator, a personal digital assistant, mobile phone, a tablet PC and a laptop. The results of both experiments are to be found in the following graphics:

The results obtained make apparent the existence of the notion of the divine proportion in those screens that most draw the attention of the senior users, specially the screens of the scientific calculators, which are similar to the size of the bank credit cards, in a horizontal position. However, at the moment of interaction there are ergonomic difficulties whether it is with holdingt he device and interacting with the small-size keyboards even if they do it with a special pen, as is the case of the personal digital assistant. Moreover, there is a kind of psychological brake, in the face of the possibility of breaking the device with which they must interact: since they regard these reduced-size devices as very small.

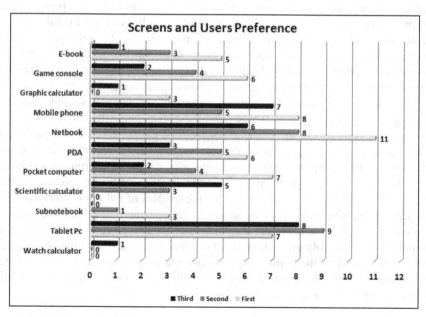

Fig. 11. The results with emulating rectangles of screens of the mobile computing

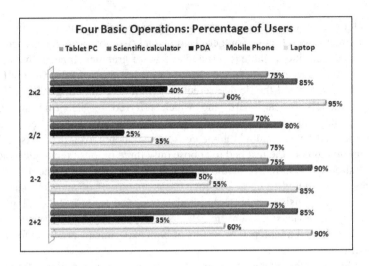

Fig. 12. Percentage of users who have carried out the four basic operations

5   Conclusion

We are immersed in a constant evolution of interaction with the microcomputing devices in the current era of communicability expansion. The users of the interactive multimedia devices and communications are split into categories. Therefore, it is important that at the moment of designing new mobile computing products aimed at the public at large the classical notions of design in the graphic arts are present, since in them persist the concepts deriving from some disciplines of the formal sciences. The advantage of the industrial design in 2D and/or 3D has been the possibility of carrying out prototypes with zero mistakes, reaching the moment of massive production. Consequently with reductions in the cost of a new productive project it is important that in this productive process the communicability expert participates from the beginning to consider the greatest possible amount of variables in the communicative process between the user and the device where the interactive system is. Focusing a great part of the financial resources of the project of a new product or service, in a continuous process of commercial marketing, through the so-called community manager experts of the social networks, can be counterproductive in the long term. The real results of the user with the interaction are the true parameters that the productive processes must follow and not the bubbles of links or contacts that can be generated and which have been the source of disappearance of endless industries at the start of the new millennium. An industrial design professional in the new millennium does not only take into account the functional aspects of the product that he/she is proposing to the community, but also the corporation image of what has been created. That is, these are professionals with a 360° vision, since they include both the aspects of the formal and the factual sciences.

Acknowledgments. A special thanks to Maria Ficarra, Carlos, Kim H. Veltman (Virtual Maastricht McLuhan Institute), and Andreas Kratky (University of Southern California) for their helps and collaboration.

References

1. Tredennick, N.: Microprocessor-Based Computer. IEEE Computer 29(10), 27–37 (1996)
2. Steane, A., Rieffel, E.: Beyond Bits: The Future of Quantum Information Processing. IEEE Computer 33(1), 38–45 (2000)
3. Bacon, D., Dam, W.: Recent Progress in Quantum Algorithms. Communications of the ACM 53(2), 84–93 (2010)
4. Salvendy, G.: Handbook of Human Factors and Ergonomics. Wiley, New Jersey (2006)
5. Bunge, M.: The science: your method and your philosophy. Siglo XXI, Buenos Aires (1981)
6. Maldonado, T.: Lo real y lo virtual. Gedisa, Barcelona (1995)
7. Osbourne, D.: Person-Centred Ergonomics: A Brantonian View Of Human Factors. Taylor & Francis, London (2004)
8. McLuhan, M.: Understanding Media. MIT Press, Massachusetts (1994)
9. Cipolla-Ficarra, F.: Evaluation of Interfaces and Portals for International E-commerce. In: International Conference on Information Systems Analysis and Synthesis – ISAS 2001, pp. 274–279. ISAS, Orlando (2001)
10. Cipolla Ficarra, F.V., Nicol, E., Cipolla Ficarra, M.: Vademecum for Innovation through Knowledge Transfer: Continuous Training in Universities, Enterprises and Industries. In: Howlett, R.J. (ed.) Innovation through Knowledge Transfer 2010. SIST, vol. 9, pp. 139–149. Springer, Heidelberg (2011)
11. Cipolla Ficarra, F.V., Nicol, E., Ficarra, V.M.: Research and Development: Business into Transfer Information and Communication Technology. In: Cipolla Ficarra, F.V., de Castro Lozano, C., Pérez Jiménez, M., Nicol, E., Kratky, A., Cipolla-Ficarra, M. (eds.) ADNTIIC 2010. LNCS, vol. 6616, pp. 44–61. Springer, Heidelberg (2011)
12. Cipolla Ficarra, F.V., Ficarra, V.M.: Software Managment Applications, Textile CAD and Human Factors: A Dreadful Industrial Example for Information and Communication Technology. In: Cipolla Ficarra, F.V., de Castro Lozano, C., Pérez Jiménez, M., Nicol, E., Kratky, A., Cipolla-Ficarra, M. (eds.) ADNTIIC 2010. LNCS, vol. 6616, pp. 121–131. Springer, Heidelberg (2011)
13. Editel: Italian Design CD-ROM. Editoria ElettronicaMilano, Milano (1995)
14. Gerhard, M., Harper, J.: Mastering Autodesk 3ds Max Design 2011. Wiley, Indianapolis (2010)
15. Cipolla-Ficarra, F.: Interazione uomo-computer nel XXI secolo: Analisi e valutazione euristica della qualità per la comunicazione e l'usabilità. Blue Herons, Bergamo (2005)
16. Raskin, J.: The Humane Interface: New Directions for Designing Interactive Systems. Addison Wesley, Reading (2000)
17. Kosslyn, S.: Image and Brain: The Resolution of the Imagery Debate. MIT Press, Massachusetts (1999)
18. Ware, C.: Information Visualization: Perception for Desing. Morgan Kaufmann Publishers, San Francisco (2000)
19. Corbalán, F.: La proporción áurea: El lenguaje matemático de la belleza. RBA, Barcelona (2010)
20. Art Gallery CD-ROM: Seatle, Microsoft (1993)

21. Le Louvre CD-ROM: Montparnasse Multimedia, Paris (1995)
22. Renoir CD-ROM: Novara: DeAgostini Multimedia (2001)
23. Cipolla-Ficarra, F.: Evaluation and Communication Techniques in Multimedia Product Design for On the Net University Education. In: Multimedia on the Net. Springer, Berlin (1996)
24. Schattschneider, D., Emmer, M.: M.C.Escher's Legacy: A Centennial Celebration. Springer, Berlin (2005)
25. Cipolla-Ficarra, F.: Quality and Communicability for Interactive Hypermedia Systems: Concepts and Practices for Design. IGI Global, Hershey (2010)

Emotion-Based Rhythmic Complexity Analysis for Automated Music Generation

Chih-Fang Huang [1] and Chi-Fang Chu [2]

[1] Department of Information Communication
Yuan Ze University, Taiwan
jeffh@saturn.yzu.edu.tw
[2] Master Program of Sound and Music Innovative Technologies
National Chiao Tung University, Taiwan
kotinal.98g@g2.nctu.edu.tw

Abstract. In the field of music emotion recognition, many researchers discuss the music features such as mode, tempo, harmony, and loudness, which significantly influence the human listening recognition result. Even though using rhythm complexity as one of the music features to analyze the music emotion is shown in the literature, it still lacks profound inquiry. In this paper, rhythm complexity is used as the key music feature to perform statistical analysis with several musical excerpts; the result is introduced into the algorithmic composition software, which automatically generates music patterns with mathematical calculation. There are two methods of rhythm complexity applied in the research, and the result shows that rhythm complexity is statistically significant correlated with music emotion arousal. Subsequently, the multiple regression analysis result is adopted into the algorithmic composition system to generate music patterns.

Keywords: Music Emotion, Music Features, Rhythm Complexity, Algorithmic Composition.

1 Introduction

The previous research shows the analysis of emotion music features theory, which can be applied to the fields of music information retrieval and psychoacoustics. Music features including tonality, tempo, loudness, articulation, pitch range, and harmony have been analyzed by researchers to differentiate their emotion states. However, to establish a music style or emotion, the rhythm complexity may be even more important in the music composition. The previous literature, including harmonic complexity [14, 9, 7, 13], melodic complexity [5, 6], and rhythm complexity [14, 5], has shown the analytical result of the mapping relations between music and emotion. Some results reveal that music with a more negative emotion will induce higher rhythm complexity [5]. This study not only references the previous research of the rhythm complexity determination, but uses the mathematical method to automatically determine the complexity with more objective criteria. Therefore the

F.V. Cipolla-Ficarra et al. (Eds.): CCGIDIS 2011, LNCS 7545, pp. 67–78, 2012.
© Springer-Verlag Berlin Heidelberg 2012

most distinguishing feature of this paper is to add the rhythm complexity into the music features as the criteria to identify the music emotion, and furthermore to perform algorithmic composition based on the result of the analysis. Fig. 1 shows the system architecture of this paper, which integrates the previous study of the theory in the emotion music features with the concept of automated composition.

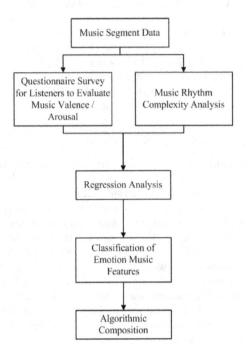

Fig. 1. System Architecture

2   Rhythm Complexity

In the previous research, rhythm complexity can be divided into performance complexity, cognitive complexity, mathematical complexities, coding complexity and information complexity, shown in the fields of psychology, physiology, musicology, computer science, and electrical engineering. The rhythm complexity that this article refers to is the cognition degree of difficulty for music rhythm by humans, or the degree of syncopation shown in the music rhythm. Thul and Toussaint's research [1, 2] shows the mathematical expression method for the rhythm complexity analysis. Livingstone and Brown's paper reveals that music rhythm is one of the important music features related to music emotion [14]. Therefore this study will use the above two methods to analyze the music rhythm complexity.

2.1   Metrical Complexity

Toussaint, G.T. presented a rhythm complexity calculation method [1] which is based on the metrical hierarchy to compute the smallest unit of each measure, and then generates the weigh table for the unit position within the measure, and finally calculate the total weight value according to the note position. In the other hand Lerdahl and Jackendoff proposed the method with the consideration of different time signatures to generate various weight tables [4]. Here we integrate both methods to calculate the rhythm complexity value based on the weight table to obtain the weight summation for all of the notes within a specific measure, and then subtract this value by the maximum weight summation that the measure can generate, to eventually get the complexity eventually. For a 16-beat measure, the onset of the typical "Clave Son" Latin music rhythm can be expressed with "x", and the rest can be represented with "." symbol, and then its weight table is shown in Fig. 2.

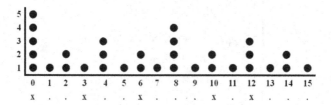

Fig. 2. Weighted Metrical Hierarchy for 16 Pulses

In this rhythmic pattern the weight summation of the note onset is $(5+1+2+2+3) =$ 13, thus the Metrical Complexity Measure can be obtained with the maximum value of the 5-note weight summation $(5+4+3+3+2) = 16$ within a measure subtracting 13 which equals 3.

2.2   Weighted Note-to-Beat Distance

Weighted Note-To-Beat Distance (WNTB) is the method to measure the rhythm complexity according to the shortest distance between note attack and strong beat [3]. With comparison to other metrical structure method such as LHL and Metrical Complexity [2], this method can calculate more rhythm complexity values of subdivisions, but the algorithm is more flexible. Due to the close relationship with strong beat, this method needs to define the strong beat position within a measure in advance; therefore, quarter notes are strong beats in 2/4, 3/4, 4/4, and 6/4 time, and eight notes are strong beats in 6/8 time.

The calculation method is as follows:

(1) Let e_i and e_{i+1} be two consecutive strong beats in a meter;
(2) Assume x is the note onset;
(3) Onset position can be in the position either before or after the strong beat e_i, but must be in the position before the next strong beat e_{i+1};

(4) Assume $T(x) = \min\{d(x,e_i), d(x,e_{i+1})\}$, d is the metrical distance between note onset and adjacent strong beat, which is a fraction defined in the operation as a meter term. For example, every note $T(x)$ is 1/2, 1/4, 1/4, 1/3, 1/3, and 1/5 respectively, as the following rhythm diagram.

(5) At last, assume n is the note number, then summate all the $D(x)$ in this measure and divide by n.

Fig. 3. Distance Metric Example

WNBD measures $D(x)$ of a note, with the definition as the following equation:

$$D(x) = \begin{cases} 0 & \text{if } x = e_i \\ 1/T(x) & \text{if } x \neq e_i \text{ ends before or at } e_{i+1} \\ 2/T(x) & \text{if } x \neq e_i \text{ ends after } e_{i+1} \\ & \quad \text{but before or at } e_{i+2} \\ 1/T(x) & \text{if } x \neq e_i \text{ ends after } e_{i+2} \end{cases} \tag{1}$$

3   Music Emotion Cognitive Space and Emotion Features Analysis

Relative to the music emotion related research, there are various experiments showing the music emotion result based on the human recognition response, and the arousal-valence two-dimensional emotion recognition space is one of the most important criteria in this field [14, 9, 12]. The paper written by Vieillard, Perez, Gosselin, Khalfa, Gagnon, and Bouchard [12] showed that the subjects who listen to music can discern four categories of music emotions, including happy, sad, scary, and peaceful, and the four kinds of music are the data source of this research.

Furthermore, in Livingstone and Brown's research [14] based on some other previous work, the 2-D quadrature coordinate system is divided into an octal form. For instance, if valence increases, then the music emotion becomes more positive, and on the other hand, if valence decreases, then the music emotion becomes more negative. When arousal is increased, then the music is more active, and if arousal goes lower, then the music emotion is becoming passive. The relationship among emotion, valence, and arousal is as in Fig. 4.

In the octal form of the music emotion classification, Livingstone and Brown used a table to summarize the mapping relationship between music feature and its correspondent emotion quadrant [14]. In this paper these important emotion features are used as the input of the algorithmic composition to generate the correspondent

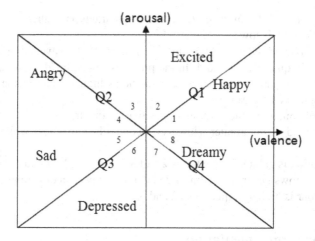

Fig. 4. 2 Dimensional Emotion Space in Octal Form

music with emotion. Therefore the main music features that the experiment uses are as follows: (Note: the bold font refers to the primary and obvious music features, and the non-bold font refers to the rarely existing music features)

Table 1. Music Feature and Its Mapping Relationship

Music feature	
Mode	**major ､ minor**
Tempo	**fast - low**
Articulation	**staccato - legato**
Pitch	**high - low**
Harmony	**simple - complex**
Loudness	**soft - loud**
Pitch Variation	large - small
Note Onset	rapid - slow
Pitch Contour	high - low

The music feature with its correspondent quadrant can be depicted in the following manner:

- For music mode, major appears in quadrants 1, 2, and 8, and the common feature of the three quadrants is the positive valence. Minor mode appears in quadrants 3, 4, and 5, and the common feature is the negative valence.
- Tempo becomes faster in the positive arousal quadrants 1, 2, 3, and 4, and slows down in the negative arousal quadrants 5, 6, 7, and 8.
- In terms of articulation, staccato shows in quadrants 1, 2, and 8, and legato shows in quadrants 4, 5, 6, and 7. Please refer to Gomez and Danuser's paper [5] to know that the positive valence area shows more staccato then the negative, and the high-arousal refers to more staccato than the low-arousal.

- In terms of pitch, the pitch in 1, 2, and 3 quadrants is higher, and the pitch in quadrants 5 and 6 is lower.
- Harmony in quadrants 1, 2, 5, and 8 is simpler, however it is shows more complexity in quadrants 3 and 4. In the previous research [5] shows that harmonic complexity is higher in the negative, and shows higher value in the high-arousal rather than in the low-arousal.
- In terms of loudness, the arousal is positive in quadrants 1, 2, 3, and 4, which means the loudness is greater. However loudness becomes less while in quadrants 5, 6, and 7.
- Pitch variation is greater in quadrants 2 and 3, but is smaller in quadrants 4 and 6.
- Note onset shows faster in quadrants 2 and 3, but slower in quadrants 5, 6, and 7.
- Pitch contour is higher in quadrants 2 and 3.

4   System Implementation

In this paper, music excerpts are used for the subjects to listen for the survey, using questionnaires for both valence and arousal, based on previous research. There are two types of rhythm complexity analysis, and the 16 subjects' valence, arousal, and rhythm complexity has been analyzed by multiple regressions. Finally music features input into the algorithmic composition system with the added rhythm complexity analysis result can be integrated to generate music automatically.

4.1   Rating

The music excerpts including 56 music segments according to the research of Vieillard et al. [12] are used as the music data for this research. There are 16 subjects listening to the music with rating for both valence and arousal from 1 to 9 points. The greater number means more active arousal and positive valence, and the smaller number refers to more passive arousal and negative valence.

16 subjects are undergraduate and graduate students coming from the Hsinchu area in Taiwan. The average age of the subjects is 21 years old, where 9 of them are male, and 7 of them are female. Most subjects have more than one year musical instrument training experience, however they are in the fields of science, engineering, electrical engineering, and computer science, not professional musicians.

4.2   Rhythm Complexity Analysis

As mentioned above, this research the rhythm complexity analysis hybrids two methods and uses Vieillard's sheet music excerpts. The time signature is given first, and then the note weight is determined. If there are two voices in the music, then we can use different calculation methods individually, and finally take the mean value. WNBD needs the strong beat position, and then we perform the WNBD measure.

4.3   Multiple Regression Analysis

Based on the above given valence and arousal data and two rhythm complexity values, SPSS (Statistical Package for Social Science) statistic tool is used for multiple-regression analysis. Metrical complexity, valence, and arousal have been analyzed with dependant variable metrical complexity and independent variables valence and arousal. In this study we find that there is a significant relationship between rhythm complexity and arousal, and this result can be found out in Fig. 5, and WNBD method shown in Fig. 6.

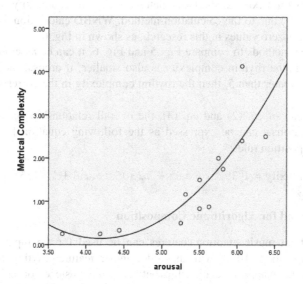

Fig. 5. The Scatter Plot of Metrical Complexity and Arousal

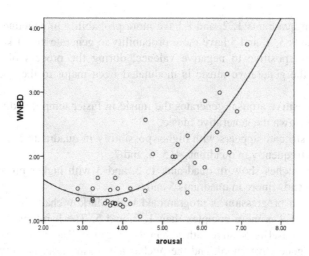

Fig. 6. The Scatter Plot of WNBD and Arousal

The regression equation of Fig. 5 is

$$Y = 0.663X^2 - 5.56X + 11.794 \tag{2}$$

The regression equation of Fig. 6 is

$$Y = 0.133X^2 - 0.901X + 2.907 \tag{3}$$

Y values in Fig. 5 and Fig. 6 represent rhythm complexity values derived from the above two methods respectively, and X represents arousal.

The Metrical Complexity method calculates the rhythm complexity of the music excerpts (see Fig. 5) due to the calculation method. WNBD calculation for the music excerpts shows less zero values in this research, as shown in Fig. 6.

With the above methods to compare Fig. 5 and Fig. 6, it can be asserted that when arousal is smaller, the rhythm complexity is also smaller; if arousal increases to be more active and greater than 5, then the rhythm complexity in the correspondent area becomes greater.

Taking the mean of eq. (2) and eq. (3), the overall relationship between rhythm complexity and arousal can be expressed as the following equation for one of the algorithmic composition rules:

$$\text{Complexity} = 0.398\text{arousal}^2 + 3.2305\text{arousal} + 7.3505 \tag{4}$$

4.4   New Method for Algorithmic Composition

The above resultant music emotion features can be used for the input data of the algorithmic composition [10, 8] with the added music feature "rhythm complexity", therefore all of the mapping relationship between the music emotion and rhythm complexity features is designed as the rule of generative music, summarized as follows:

- Mode: data in quadrants 1, 2, and 8 have more probability to generate major key, and in quadrants 3, 4, and 5 have more probability to generate minor key. If it is in transition from positive to negative valence, during the process of algorithmic composition the generative music is modulated from major to the relative minor key.
- Tempo: the positive arousal generates the music in faster tempo, and the negative arousal slows down the generative music.
- Articulation: staccato appears with higher possibility in quadrants 1, 2, and 8, and legato shows frequently in quadrants 4, 5, 6, and 7.
- Pitch: higher pitches show in quadrants 1, 2, and 3 with higher probability, and lower pitches show more in quadrants 5 and 6.
- Harmony: chord progression is programmed with Markov chain. The harmony in quadrants 3 and 4 is more complex than 1, 2, and 5. The harmony complexity is higher while arousal is positive rather than the negative. The generative melody is based on the generative chord, and the pitches are mostly selected from the chord notes.

- Loudness: the positive arousal will cause greater loudness. On the contrary the negative arousal will increase the loudness.
- Pitch Variation: it generates more pitch variation in quadrants 2 and 3, less in 4 and 6.
- Pitch Contour: it shows higher in quadrants 2 and 3.
- Rhythm Complexity: when arousal is negative, rhythm complexity is lower; when arousal is positive, rhythm complexity is higher.

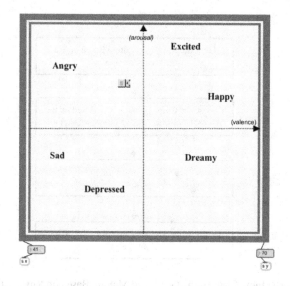

Fig. 7. Algorithmic Composition GUI with Emotion and Rhythm Complexity Using Max/MSP Program

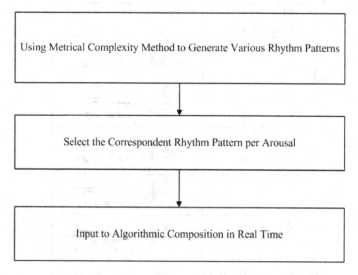

Fig. 8. The Flow Chart of the Automated Composition with Rhythm Complexity Input

Finally, the above mentioned music features are sent to the Max/MSP program [11] to perform the real-time calculation for the algorithmic composition. As shown in Fig. 7, the system can generate music based on the input of the cursor position as the emotion features. The emotion and rhythm complexity based algorithmic composition system, as shown in Fig. 8, can be implemented.

Fig. 9 shows the flow chart of the generated melody based on rhythm complexity. The automated generated melody is based on not only the rhythm complexity, but also the sieve theory [15] filtering out the unwanted pitch notes to establish the diatonic scale.

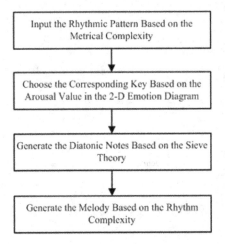

```
Input the Rhythmic Pattern Based on the
Metrical Complexity

        ↓

Choose the Corresponding Key Based on the
Arousal Value in the 2-D Emotion Diagram

        ↓

Generate the Diatonic Notes Based on the Sieve
Theory

        ↓

Generate the Melody Based on the Rhythm
Complexity
```

Fig. 9. The Flow Chart of the Generated Melody Based on Rhythm Complexity

Metrical Complexity	Pattern
1	
2	
3	
4	
5	

Fig. 10. Generative Rhythm Complexity Pattern Examples

The various generative rhythm patterns, as shown in Fig. 10, are based on the Metrical Complexity method inversely, which can be used as the generative music rhythm database.

5   Conclusion

This research integrates emotion features with the algorithmic composition concept, and adds the rhythm complexity analysis result to not only enrich the computer generated music content, but also to create a novel and pioneer way to perform automated composition without complicated music parametric input, compared with the previous research. The rhythm patterns can be successfully generated according to the rhythm complexity analysis result using statistic multiple-regression method; therefore the proposed method can be used in the field of automated composition to compose a melodic line with generative pitches accordingly. In the future, other rhythm complexity methods can be used in the system, and brainwave cognitive analysis can be also applied to make the system analysis more completely.

Acknowledgment. The authors would like to appreciate the support from National Science Council projects of Taiwan: NSC99-2410-H-155 -035 -MY2.

References

1. Thul, E., Toussiant, G.T.: On the Relation between Rhythm Complexity Measures. In: Proceedings of the Canadian Conference on Computer Science and Software Engineering, Montreal, Quebec, Canada, pp. 1–9 (2008)
2. Thul, E., Toussiant, G.T.: Analysis of Musical Rhythm Complexity Measures in a Cultural Context. In: Proceedings of the Canadian Conference on Computer Science and Software Engineering, Montreal, Canada, May 12-13, pp. 1–9 (2008)
3. Gómez, F., Melvin, A., Rappaport, D., Toussaint, G.T.: Mathematical measures of syncopation. In: BRIDGES: Mathematical Connections in Art, Music and Science, Banff, Alberta, Canada, July 31 - August 3, pp. 73–84 (2005)
4. Lerdahl, F., Jackendoff, R.: A Generative Theory of Tonal Music. MIT Press, Cambridge (1983)
5. Balkwill, L.L., Thompson, W.F.: A Cross-Cultural Investigation of the Perception of Emotion in Music. Music Perception: An Interdisciplinary Journal 17(1), 43–64 (1999)
6. Balkwill, L.L., Thompson, W.F., Matsunaga, R.: Recognition of emotion in Japanese, Western, and Hindustani music by Japanese listeners. Japanese Psychological Research 46(4), 337–349 (2004)
7. Meyer, L.B.: Emotion and Meaning in Music. The University of Chicago Press (1956)
8. Supper, M.: A Few Remarks on Algorithmic Composition. Computer Music Journal 25(1), 48–53 (2001)
9. Gomez, P., Danuser, B.: Relationships Between Musical Structure and Psychophysiological Measures of Emotion. Emotion American Psychological Association 7(2), 377–387 (2007)
10. Winsor, P.: Automated Music Composition. University of North Texas Press (1992)

11. Bowe, R.: Interactive Music Systems: Machine Listening and Composing. MIT Press, Cambridge (1992)
12. Vieillard, S., Peretz, I., Gosselin, N., Khalfa, S., Gagnon, L., Bouchard, B.: Happy, sad, scary and peaceful musical excerpts for research on emotions. Cognition & Emotion 22(4), 720–752 (2008)
13. Livingstone, S.R., Muhlberger, R., Brown, A.R., Thompson, W.F.: Changing musical emotion: A computational rule system for modifying score and performance. Computer Music Journal 34(1), 41–64 (2010)
14. Livingston, S.R., Brown, A.R.: Dynamic Response: Real-Time Adaptation for Music Emotion. In: Proceedings of the Australasian Conference on Interactive Entertainment, Sydney, pp. 105–111 (2005)
15. Xenakis, I., Rahn, J.: Sieves. Perspectives of New Music 28(1), 58–78 (1990)

Computer Graphics for Students of the Factual Sciences

Francisco V. Cipolla Ficarra[1,2], Valeria M. Ficarra[2], and Andreas Kratky[3]

HCI Lab. – F&F Multimedia Communications Corp.
[1] ALAIPO: Asociación Latina de Interacción Persona-Ordenador
[2] AINCI: Asociación Internacional de la Comunicación Interactiva
c/ Angel Baixeras, 5 – AP 1638, 08080 Barcelona, Spain
Via Pascoli, S. 15 – CP 7, 24121 Bergamo, Italy
[3] University of Southern California – Interactive Media Division, School Cinematic Arts
900 West 34th Street, SCA 213 – Los Angeles, CA 90089-2211, USA
ficarra@alaipo.com, info@ainci.com, akratky@cinema.usc.edu

Abstract. We present the main qualities that icons in interactive systems for graphic computing must possess for students of the social sciences and/or user unfamiliar with the 2D and 3D representation of reality through emulation and simulation with personal computers. In the current work we will analyze the interfaces of a software to generate animated and static graphics, which have evolved jointly with the operating system and the graphic hardware. Besides, a series of strategies are presented in the college teaching unrelated to the computer graphics sector.

Keywords: Computer Graphics, Computer Animation, Quality, Interface, Iconography, Education, Software, 3D Studio.

1 Introduction

In the history of the labs and the college research centres, the graphics computing environment has been essential for the development of the hypermedia, human-computer interaction, virtual reality, etc. [1] [2] [3] Some college centres of Southern Europe, for instance, focused in the early 90s on computing basics such as programming, algorithms, databases, natural languages, etc. and those whotried to include the design of interactive systems without encompassing the communicability aspects and graphic computing have seen many research and development projects fail. Now those in graphic computing who intended to stay at the top of the pyramid to dictate dogmas to be followed in the field of interactive design, have also fallen to the democratic advance of the users in the pixels sector, thanks to the worldwide circulation of commercial programmes. One of them, the Autodesk 3D Studio Max [4] which will be analyzed in the current work, joined to the MS-Windows operating system on the computers of millions of users, generated a tsunami process in the democratization of the artistic and scientific pixel.

F.V. Cipolla-Ficarra et al. (Eds.): CCGIDIS 2011, LNCS 7545, pp. 79–93, 2012.
© Springer-Verlag Berlin Heidelberg 2012

Since the 80s Microsoft started to market Windows worldwide. Those were years in which computers had a solid and important market with IBM. Nevertheless, since the classic MS-DOS with its command line until the Windows 3.1 or '95 Windows one sees how the user of small computers has intensified the consumption of the products of this brand. This combination of interaction with the computers, whether it is through commands or pop-up menus was transferred into the early lines of 3D Studio. One of the reasons for the expansion of the Microsoft products in Southern Europe was the cost of the clone computers compatible with the IBM PC which made the quality or the prestige of a brand stay in the background [5].

Other operating systems belonging to the environment of Apple were not accepted by most of the Spanish-speaking users in Europe and Latin America. This was due to a great extent to the cost factor of the hardware and of some specific applications in their origins, although the quality of the operating system and of its applications has always been excellent. Here is one of the historic reasons that can make a whole community plump for a kind of operative system or another, which evidently has an influence on the hardware [5]. The purchasing power of the communities still sets patterns in the computer consumer market, and in the division of the users by the technological divide. A factor that in the research and development labs of the last decades of the past century was not very present. They kept on planning and developing products and services for users of the great cities, without restraints in the purchasing power.

The idea in the 80s by Nicholas Negroponte [6] of merging television, print and computer science towards a "computer-based multimedia technology" was already a reality with Windows '98. The democratization of the Internet and the appearance of the knowbots are some aspects of this era of commercial computing which will erupt in the early years of the 21st century. The influence of these facts is such that the new operating system had many of its screens structured in the same way as the Internet Explorer. It was a way to "force" the users so that they assimilated the need to be wired to the Internet. Quickly the new versions of 3D Studio also adjusted to these new interfaces and the possibility of working on-line. The operating systems of the 90s remained the cornerstones of this decade as it has happened since the 80s in the "domestic" software environment.

2   Operating Systems and Commercial Graphic Software

There are many Autodesk products which have developed during the international momentum of the MS-DOS. These were products such as AutoCAD, Animator and even the early versions of the 3D Studio which served to diffusion the computer science related to the animated graphics and all its derivations [7]. The advent of new operating systems such as Windows NT or Windows '95 did not pose any problem to those users who were accustomed to working with Autodesk products since the compatibility of the software has always been 100% with a high reliability level of the results. The new version of the operating system does not generate any problem either for the correct functioning of the 3D Studio Max 2.5 as it can be seen in the screen of the figures 1, 2 and 3. In the first we see how a rendering made in a quarter of the first course of computer science students in a college of Catalan design with the MS-DOS version of 3D Studio and in the third its incorporation in the Windows version of the 3D Studio, without this operation generating any loss of information due to the compatibility of the software.

There are many Autodesk products which have developed during the international momentum of the MS-DOS. These were products such as AutoCAD, Animator and even the early versions of the 3D Studio which served to democratize the computer science related to the animated graphics and all its derivations. The advent of new operative systems such as Windows NT or Windows '95 did not pose any problem to those users who were accustomed to working with Autodesk products since the compatibility of the software has always been 100% with a high reliability level of the results. The new version of the operative system does not generate any problem either for the correct functioning of the 3D Studio Max 2.5 as it can be seen in the screen of the figures 1, 2 and 3. In the first we see how a rendering made in a quarter of the first course of computer science students in a college of Catalan design with the MS-DOS version of 3D Studio and in the third its incorporation in the Windows version of the 3D Studio, without this operation generating any loss of information due to the compatibility of the software.

Fig. 1. Students without any previous experience made a five-minutes long animation where a cow creates a virtual beer and drinks it after (1995-1996). On the computer screen we can see the interface of the 3D Studio in MS-DOS version.

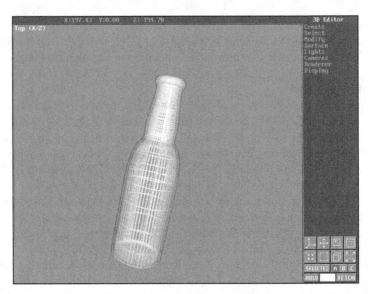

Fig. 2. Interface with icons which would be kept along the versions, as they appear in the lower right angle

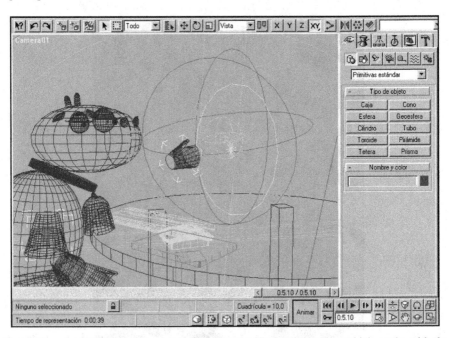

Fig. 3. Transfer of the animation project to the new 3D Studio version which works with the Windows '98 version. On it can be seen the wealth of icons of the graphic interface.

Thanks to the compatibility of the software, the architecture, animation, television, cinema studios etc., can keep on working with the earlier versions, whereas the staff gets acquainted with the breakthroughs contributed in the new versions of the graphic software. Another of the reasons to work with the former versions is due to the fact that there are many objects that can be stored in a kind of catalogue, in order to be recycled in new projects. This is another quality aspect of commercial graphic software: reusability. These objects generally can be related to the indoors decoration of a building or its outdoors appearance. "Classical" examples were the CD-ROMs *3D Props [8] and 3D Residential* [9] which can even today be incorporated in many three-dimensional scenes or the "modern" products stored in the *World Creating Toolkit* which went with the last 20th century versions of the 3 D Studio Max [4]. In this latter CD-ROM there are over 600 Mb of objects, shapes, scenes, animations, sounds, materials, etc., which could be visualized in a fast way with the *Asset Manager* from 3D Studio Max. In few words, the possibility of carrying out 2D and 3D objects, profiting from the compatibility and reusability of the software for the free circulation or not of the end products has allowed to also increase the democratization process of the pixel among inexperienced users.

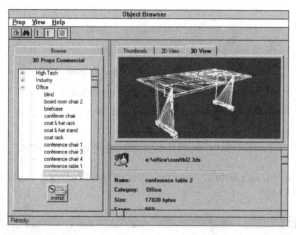

Fig. 4. Transfer of the animation project to the new 3D Studio version which works with the Windows '98 version. On it can be seen the wealth of icons of the graphic interface.

3   Quality Attributes in the Hypermedia Systems

The accessibility of the information in the multimedia systems is one of the most important attributes for navigation, since it directly affects orientation, that is, knowing where one is and from that place knowing the different alternatives to visit other nodes [10]. What nowadays is something common in the Internet, mobile multimedia phones, etc. in the 90s was a design attribute that was supposed to be included in the making of the project, realization and evaluation of the hypermedia systems. However, in an on-line or off-line interactive system the inexpert user may have available a good orientation (an essential quality attribute since the early interactive systems such as the hypertext systems) but can't have access to the requested information due to failings in the design or in the hyperbase. Besides, in that decade a similarity was seen in the interactive multimedia systems to other computer systems in regard to the main types of access to the information. The accessibility to the information stored in a hyperbase is basically through:

- Index or menu (early versions of the 3D Studio which worked with the MS-DOS).
- Outline (The CD-ROMs bookshops 3D Props and 3D Residential [8], [9] with 3D objects compatible with other programmes of the international commercial graphic software).
- Direct search (in some screens of 3D Studio)

Nevertheless, it is possible to find a combination of these types of access as it can be seen in index and direct search examples, or rather index, outline and direct search, in the different options that make up the 3D studio application and the different marketing manes it has had along time. Schematically, the evolution of the product and its denomination can be depicted in the following way:

> ↳ **3D Studio MS-DOS (releases 1, 2, 3 and 4): 1990 - 1994**
> ↪ **3D Studio Max (releases 1, 2 and 3): 1996 - 1999**
> ↪ **Discreeet 3D Max (releases 4, 5, 6 and 7): 2000 - 2004**
> ↪ **Autodesk 3D Studio Max (releases 8 and 9): 2005 - 2006**
> ↳ **Autodesk 3D Studio Max 2008, 2009, 2010, and 2011**

Fig. 5. History of the evolution of the denomination used commercial software

A greater level of accessibility can be seen in the following examples of off-line multimedia [10] [11]:

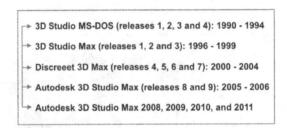

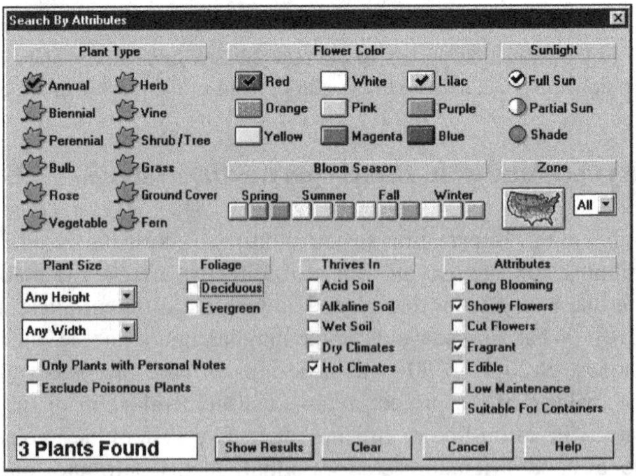

Fig. 6. Over 50 attributes or boolean connectors (and) for the search of an information

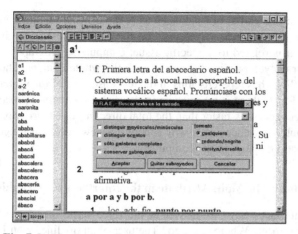

Fig. 7. In the search attributes is included the used typography

Direct search modalities have required a long learning process by the expert users, since there are many options and the mnemonic factor of usability engineering, was not considered in the early versions of 3D Studio (figure 2). The product was aimed at expert users. However, the evolution of the operating system and Internet have brought it closer to the inexpert users. Inexperienced users who had great difficulty at the moment of having access to the information writing commands such as was MS-DOS.

In contrast, the factual function observes the direct communication in the human-computer interaction process without the generation of mistakes [10] [13]. Direct communication is is carried out from the keyboard (there are other means for direct communication in the human-computer interaction, such as: the microphone, when the application has the goal of teaching languages or a video camera in the teleconferences via Internet, just to mention two examples) and which belongs to the highest level of interdependence in the dynamic process of the user-computer communication. In this attribute the meaning-significant relationship of the words is not considered, but the direct communication channel. However, in the direct communication the treatment of the mistakes n case they exist can be seen, that is, the different kinds of help, the final blockage of the functioning of the system, keeping the graphic project before reinitiating the computer, etc.

It is in the factual function where the contact between the user and the computer makes the issue of emulation or simulation of reality in the metaphor of the interface take a second place (the naturalness of the metaphor is another quality attribute of the interactive systems [13], since the interaction is carried out with the writing of letters and symbols. There are systems which exceptionally admit the use of some punctuation signs for Boolean operations. In the case of the keyboard, the user has access to the hyperbase [14] by writing the letters in a frame that simulates a line of commands (as in the Unix operative system or MS-DOS).

The words that are typed in must not necessarily have a previous meaning. As one starts to write the name of a node possible options start to appear. The direct access to the hyperbase may be partial or total, such as in the off-line scientific encyclopaedias for the wider public. In some encyclopaedias, the direct access of the hyperbase may be partial since it is related to a specific issue: computers, geography, maths, etc. In contrast in other encyclopaedias the access is to the whole content. The difference in the access modalities has repercussions in the response time of the system on what the user is looking for. If there is no mistake in the direct interaction process, the partial modality of direct access is faster than the total direct access. Currently the studies in the brain computer interfaces area will generate a new software range to carry out animated and static graphics in the computer.

3.1   Orientation: The Main Attribute in the Interfaces for Graphic Design

Traditionally interfaces have to answer to the three basic questions: Where am I? Where do I come from? Where can I go? The user of an off-line or on-line interactive system is grateful for a fast answer to keep on sailing through the contents.

Now in the context of the graphic interfaces, the appearance of menus on the screen, pop-up menus, etc. makes even the experienced user lose the orientation inside the working area. If we take a look at the early versions of 3D Studio for MS-DOS we can see that the pop-up menus were concentrated on the upper area, those belonging to file commands (file, edit, select, etc.) similar to what happened with the office automation programmes, such as Wordperfect, Lotus 1-2-3, etc.

Whereas those commands related to graphic computing were concentrated in the right area of the screen. The possibility of mobility of those vertical command bars was of special interest, not only because of ergonomy reasons among the left-handed users, including ambidextrous people, but out of cultural reasons, in places where reading is from left to right, for instance [15].

Also the entry or exit peripherals could be personalized. With the versions that were working in the Windows environment, the user had great freedom to personalize his/her working area. A personalization that went from the size of the icons, the size of the text in the assists, the thickness of the lines, etc.

4   Icons: Emulation or Simulation of Reality?

An agile way to move inside an interactive system for the realization of static and dynamic graphics is through the direct access icons, many of which depict commands that are inside the pop-up windows. In the figure 8 were presented with (*) and (?) the icons since this interface has been used in the experiments carried out with inexperienced users such that they write what operation or command can be associated to it. As it can be seen, in some of them is noticeable a small triangle in the right bottom part, which means that other icons pop-up as it can be seen in the figure 8 (number 1).

For the computer-savvy user of the 90s some of the icons which appear on the upper bar of figure 8 (*) are easy to recognize in their function, regardless whether they have or not knowledge of graphic computing or have worked with other similar products. Others in contrast for theoreticians of graphic computing who haven't previously used this software, may find their meaning ambiguous (?). Consequently, these are icons which do not derive from a labour sector related to it. Besides, the great problem of these icons is that there has been no international homologation of them. See in annex #1 some commercial software screens of the new millennium where some icons have stayed identical among themselves through time and are those which refer to the basic files operations, etc. Now in the upper bar it is feasible to group them in two sets of a greater or lesser degree of ambiguity. In the first group would be those whose meaning can be intuited aprioristically, such as those that bear the symbol (*). In the second group we have the most complex ones (?). These two groups have been shaped along the years in experiments with expert users and non-expert in computer science.

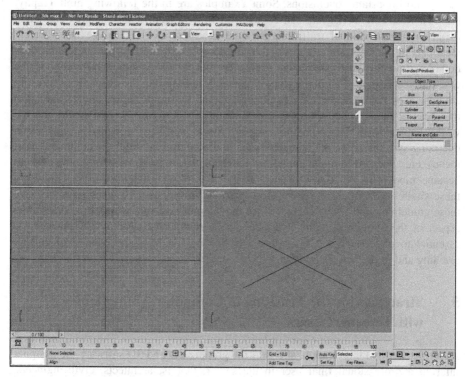

Fig. 8. A strategy followed by the commercial software 3D Studio Max (release 7) to indicate that there is a listing of them on that icon. The home page has 62 options for direct access with icons.

When a user doesn't know the meaning of an icon or command, in the 80s and 90s said user resorted as a rule to the help handbook in paper or digital support inside the programme itself. The illustrated examples that these helps contained, made easier the understanding of the meaning and function of it. Other users went for explorative navigation without looking up these helps. In relation to this kind of classical navigation of the multimedia systems in the 90s in the new millennium some call it snake because of the movement in the shape of 'x' or 'y' on the computer screen, without making any reference to explorative navigation, which already existed in the 90s. [13] Not mentioning the sources of information or not knowing the history of computer science and all the disciplines that derive from it only helps to generate more confusion in the interactive design and this usually stems from the field of humanistic computer science.

In the human-computer interaction and the human-computer communication is where the anthropologists, social communicators, sociologists, semiotics or semiologists, scholars of the cultural systems, usability engineers, etc., have gathered information about the different meanings of the images that many times were laid on the menus, mobile phones keys, etc. In the mid 90s with the democratization of the Internet and the generation of McLuhan's global village, interesting studies were made with important conclusions. Some examples are in the following bibliography: [15-19]. Research works that started with the comparison of the pictures and static images, in the shape of traffic signs, hand gestures, etc. to analyze the different meanings in the different cultures and trying to establish the first parameters in icons homologation. In these parameters they tried that the icons simulated reality in the case that the degree of ambiguity was practically null among the different cultures. In contrast, they resorted to reality emulation, agreed by the designers and explained in the areas of helps, when there was no relationship between the real world and the world depicted on the computer screen. Some software companies that made operating systems, upon realizing mistakes in the interpretation of the command bars, menus, etc., decided to make guidelines for the software programmers. Some of them became models to be followed such as the Macintosh guidelines [20]. Obviously those studies were focused on a historic period. However, it is mistaken to criticize those guidelines in the new century since they do not take into account the diachronic aspect of the evolution of the interfaces in the interactive systems. Diachronism is essential to understand the main mistakes that are made in the context of college teaching and in the new technologies [5].

5   Strategies for the Teaching of Computer Animations with Unexpert Users

As a rule, in this kind of applications of the graphic 2D and 3D software the designer inferred a professional final user in the sector, that is, architects, civil engineers, multimedia technicians, etc. That is, the animation system per analyzed computer was not planned for the rookie computer user, and much less so in graphic computing. Nevertheless, there are academic realities which placed many Catalan students of journalism/audio-visual, for instance, in front of a computer with this software in MS-DOS version with software and help handbooks in English, and with college professors hired with the so-called garbage contracts, that is, the minimum legal salary, per hour, and not renewable after two courses. Besides, for many of these students it was the first time that they interacted with a computer. The strategy followed was a compiling of personalized information of the previous knowledge of the use of the computer through an anonymous questionnaire. The questionnaire was made up of closed and open questions (it was important to get the greatest possible information from the potential users of graphic software, as for previous experiences, tastes, preferences, etc. in the multimedia context). In this questionnaire they were asked if they used the computer, if they knew the office automation programmes, the kind of computer that PC was or laptop (commercial brand of worldwide circulation or clone), which were the peripherals wired to it (modem, printer, scanner, CD/DVD reader, etc.), if they used it for the videogames (types of videogames), if they knew how to program, if they had knowledge of self-editing programmes, etc. They were also asked their knowledge of the fledgling audiovisual 2D and/or 3D industry for television and cinema, for instance. Later on the image on figure 9 was projected and the users had to write the meaning of the icons in a blank sheet, placing the names and surnames in each sheet. Through the open questions of the questionnaire and the description of the icons it was already known what was the level of previous knowledge in the use of the computer of the students.

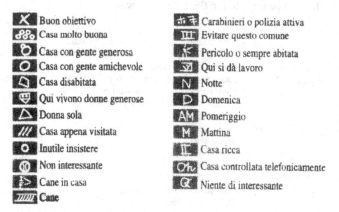

Fig. 9. Icons which appeared painted on the façades of the houses by the potential thieves, in some villages of the Bergamasque Alps (Lombardia, Italy). In the end, the revelation of the meaning of each one of them favoured the communication inside the classroom between the students and the professor.

Starting from the compiled information, groups were formed for the practices in the lab, placing expert and non-expert users in each one of the work groups. Simultaneously they started with the teaching of the basic concepts of graphic computing in master classes with first simple practices in the lab computers, such as making 2D figures and the first three-dimensional objects in a set. That is, all the groups inside the lab had to make synchronically the same operations that the professor made.

It was mandatory to pass the mouse and the keyboard on among the members of the group every five minutes. Once the members of the group had acquired the basic knowledge of 2D and 3D the need arose to make a script or storyboard of a computer animation. In that direction were presented works selected in the computer animation festivals such as Immagina in France, Siggraph in USA, college works awarded in contests, films and television series. In all of them there was an attempt to explain the four cardinal points of an excellent computer animation: originality, simplicity, universality and humour. The scripts were made as extra curricular activities, they were discussed with each group and once approved they went on with the making of said films. Obviously with a professor and a technical assistant for 25 inexperienced students in the use of the computers, without knowledge of English for the handbooks, it was very difficult to reach that objective of the computer animations within the teaching schedule. One only has to think of how long the rendering process took once the animations were made. In that reality the technical assistant had many extra hours in his monthly salary. In the first stage of carrying out small practical works in a single synchronized working group, the problems derived from the complexity of the interface, the commands, their functions, etc., were easily overcome by the inexperienced users. The problem came up when they didn't have aid mechanisms in an autonomous way because of language reasons –English) and the small number of professors and/or technicians in the lab in agreement with the planned hours in the curricula (80 hours). Schematically this can be depicted in the following way:

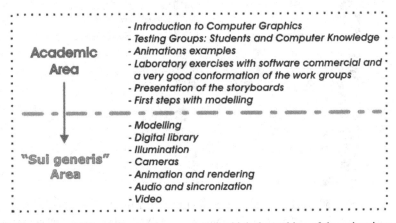

Fig. 10. The horizontal line indicates the moment at which the making of the animations meant extra hours for the lab assistant

In few words, the inexperienced users were capable of assimilating quickly the theoretical concepts of 2D, 3D, the main principles of animation, making synchronized group practices, making a story board in agreement with the cardinal quality points in an animation. However, once the project had started and had been partially developed. The last day devoted to the animation project they came to the lab and they found the .mov file (QuickTime video), that is, the animation, in their intranet work file.

6   Lessons Learned

The 3D commercial graphic software that we have analyzed in the current work can be quickly assimilated even by non-experienced computer users stemming from the social sciences such as   journalism and/or audiovisual students in the Catalan case. The dynamics of the work group with the whole class in the same project simultaneously is very positive even in the case where there is no previous knowledge of the software. However, this modality of work makes the users who were for the first time in front of a computer screen to generate static and/or animated graphics overcome their fear. Besides, not knowing the meaning of the icons, pop-up menus, etc. which were written in English, the same as the help in digital and paper support. That is, in this educational context, the usability problem was compounded by a severe communicability problem in the interaction with the interactive system. This was an interactive system which worked in the MS-DOS platform and in which the help was not aimed at the rookie users. Besides, the execution of certain commands was made directly from the keyboard, thus increasing the possibility of making mistakes. Now in an interface of these systems having all the alternatives open generates fear of disorientation on the part of the users, and loss of the work done. Many times in the face of the disorientation and the lack of an error message or some kind of feedback of the interactive systems led to reinitializing the computer, especially when the waiting took some minutes. However, this kind of software required a powerful hardware, since the synthesis images it makes entail carrying out many calculations per second. This time considerably increased the rendering process, before getting the final animation, for instance, which is obviously part of a set of technical issues that were ignored by the organizers of the academic courses. Aside from this circumstance, those who started to work with this software and kept on with it along time have participated directly or indirectly in the democratization of the pixel in Southern Europe.

7   Conclusion

A way to speed up and spread software to generate 2D and 3D graphics internationally along thirty years is to keep constant those areas of work that the user uses frequently. In this sense, the analyzed software has been capable of finding the ideal solutions for the specialized users, with the material editor, trendering, animation management, etc. Now in the software for computer animations it is usual to resort to the merging of several modalities to interact with it, that is, menu bars, buttons with icons, etc. When we see that an icon has its title written on it or when by placing the cursor on it the name or the function appears, that phenomenon tells of communicability problems that have repercussions on the usability of the system, regardless of the user who interacts with it. The quality attributes have been progressively incorporated into the interfaces of the different versions. However, this adaptation process in the era of the expansion of communicability is slow, because of the great current evolution of the potential users who are interested in carrying out computer animations in the shortest possible time. Another of the problems detected in this kind of software is the lack of an iconographic homogeneity or ISO guidelines in the relation between meaning and the significant, of those icons who fulfil the same function. In principle, this lack of emulation of reality has also been transferred to the multimedia phones and other microcomputing devices. Consequently, there is a certain return to the 90s with the explorative navigation of the interface and the need of evaluating again the cultural aspects of the different societies prior to generating interactive systems for graphic computing with a worldwide circulation.

Acknowledgments. A special thanks to Maria Ficarra, Luisa Varela, Doris Edison, Jim Carré, Pamela Fulton, Emma Nicol (University of Strathclyde) and Carlos for their helps.

References

1. Popovic, Z.: Controlling Physics in Realistic Character Animation. Communication of ACM 43(7), 50–58 (2000)
2. Vasconcelos, N.: From Pixels to Semantic Spaces: Advances in Content-Based Image Retrieval. IEEE Computer 40(7), 20–26 (2007)
3. Grahan, T., Grau, O.: Virtual Graphics for Broadcast Production. IEEE Computer 42(7), 42–47 (2009)
4. Gerhard, M., Harper, J., McFarland, J.: Mastering Autodesk 3ds Max Design 2010. Wisley, Indianapolis (2009)
5. Cipolla-Ficarra, F., Cipolla-Ficarra, M.: Interactive Systems, Design and Heuristic Evaluation: The Importance of the Diachronic Vision. In: Tsihrintzis, G.A., Virvou, M., Howlett, R.J., Jain, L.C. (eds.) New Directions in Intelligent Interactive Multimedia Systems and Services - 2. Studies in Computational Intelligence, vol. 142, pp. 625–634. Springer, Heidelberg (2009)
6. Negroponte, N.: Being Digital. Knopf, New York (1996)
7. Cipolla Ficarra, F.V., Alma, J., Cipolla-Ficarra, M.: Behaviour Computer Animation, Communicability and Education for All. In: Stephanidis, C. (ed.) HCII 2011 and UAHCI 2011, Part IV. LNCS, vol. 6768, pp. 538–547. Springer, Heidelberg (2011)
8. 3D Props Commercial CD-ROM. Autodesk, San Rafael (1995)
9. 3D Residential CD-ROM. Autodesk, San Rafael (1995)
10. Cipolla-Ficarra, F.: Evaluation of Multimedia Components. In: Proc. IEEE Multimedia Conference on Multimedia Computing Systems, Ottawa, pp. 557–564 (1997)
11. Garden Encyclopedia CD-ROM. Book that Work, Palo Alto (1996)
12. Diccionario de la Lengua Española CD-ROM. Espasa-Calpe, Madrid (1996)
13. Cipolla-Ficarra, F.: Communicability Design and Evaluation in Cultural and Ecological Multimedia Systems. In: Proc. MSCommunicability 2008, pp. 1–8. ACM Press, New York (2008)
14. Tompa, F.: A Data Model for Flexible Hypertext Database System. ACM Transactions on Information Systems 1, 85–100 (1989)
15. Fernandes, T.: Global Interface Design: A Guide to Designing International User Interfaces. Academic Press, Boston (1995)
16. White, G.: Designing for the Last Billion. Interactions 15(1), 56–58 (2008)
17. Wachs, J., Kolsch, M., Stern, H., Edan, Y.: Vision-Based Hand-Gesture Applications. Communications of ACM 54(2), 60–71 (2011)
18. Hornecker, E.: The Role of Physicality in Tangible and Embodied Interactions. Interactions 18(2), 19–23 (2011)
19. Agrawala, M., Li, W., Berthouzoz, F.: Design Principles for Visual Communication. Communications of ACM 54(4), 60–69 (2011)
20. Apple: Macintosh Human Interface Guidelines. Addison-Wesley, Massachusetts (1992)

Annex #1

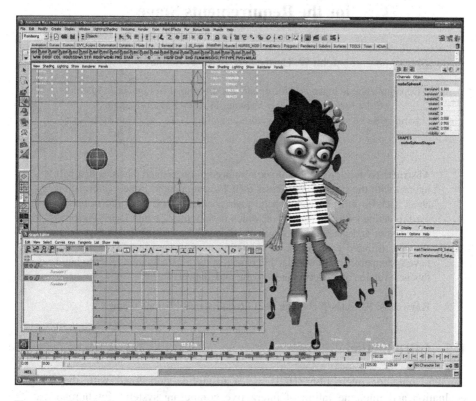

Fig. 11. Autodesk Maya 2008 interface. We have the same software house (Maya and 3D Max) but the icons very are differents (see figure 8).

Extension of Personas Technique
for the Requirements Stage

John W. Castro and Silvia T. Acuña

Departamento de Ingeniería Informática, Universidad Autónoma de Madrid
Calle Francisco Tomás y Valiente 11, 28049 Madrid, Spain
john.castro@estudiante.uam.es, silvia.acunna@uam.es

Abstract. To develop usable software we need to understand the users that will interact with the system. Personas is a HCI technique that gathers information about users in order to comprehend their characteristics. This information is used to define fictitious persons on which development should focus. Personas provides an understanding of the user, often overlooked in SE developments. We aim to improve requirements elicitation through the use of Personas. We have systematized and formalized Personas in the SE tradition in order to build this new version of the technique into the requirements stage.

Keywords: Personas Technique, HCI, Requirements Elicitation Stage.

1   Introduction

Human-Computer Interaction (HCI) as "a discipline concerned with the design, evaluation and implementation of interactive computing systems for human use..." [3]. This involves studying and getting acquainted with people as members of groups or organizations, the conditions under which subjects are likely to want to use their device, as well as the characteristics involved in this interaction. HCI processes and techniques assure that the output software product conforms to the minimum usability standards.

HCI techniques typically have two shortcomings that restrain their use within SE (Software Engineering) processes [5]. On the one hand, they do not have a well-defined, complete and detailed procedure to guide the software engineer through the proper application of the technique. On the other hand, they do not prescribe products output by applying the techniques.

The Personas technique [7] gathers, analyses and synthesizes information related to the users that are to interact with the software system. It helps to focus software analysis and design on the end user features and goals. However, it shares the above shortcomings of HCI techniques: it has no detailed definition of activities and products. These problems make the introduction of Personas into the SE requirements stage overly complex and unclear for developers.

According to HCI, there should be an understanding not only of users' needs and goals but also of their characteristics and capabilities in order to design and

F.V. Cipolla-Ficarra et al. (Eds.): CCGIDIS 2011, LNCS 7545, pp. 94–103, 2012.

implement a usable system [1]. The understanding of the people that interact with the system should constitute the groundwork for software development. The SE requirements activity could be improved by incorporating the Personas technique tasks to understand the user. The goal of our research is to modify Personas to readily build the technique into the requirements stage of regular SE developments.

This paper is structured as follows. Section 2 describes the Personas technique, discussing the power of this technique, and its limitations. In Section 3 we analyse how to align Personas with SE and present a modification of Personas, together with some examples of the products to be generated. Section 4 discusses the impact of building Personas into the requirements stage. Finally, Section 5 addresses the conclusions.

2   The Personas Technique: Strengths and Weaknesses

Personas is attributed to Alan Cooper [6], who later updated the method in [5] and [7]. On this groundwork, several versions [9], [11] have been proposed for successfully generating *personas,* the main final product output by the technique. To assure that users' viewpoints are the focus during software design, the Personas technique creates fictitious users called *personas* rather than taking into account the real users. The personas characterize the target users on whom development efforts should focus. The main benefit of Personas is to determine whom the development should target.

Personas is a powerful and multi-purpose analysis technique that can help software engineers to identify the functionalities of the software system. Both the personas' goals and tasks are essential for this purpose [7]. Developers that design for particular personas (thanks to having used Personas technique), even if they are fictional:

- Design for the end user, assuring that they do not project their own goals, motivations, skills and mental models on the software system development.
- Prioritize functionalities, assuring that they do not build functionalities that future users might never use. For example, the developer might wonder, "Does Sandra need to do this operation very often?" The response to questions like these helps to prioritize the functions that the software system should have based on its users.

We tried to apply Cooper's version of the Personas technique [7] and we came up against the following obstacles. The first step of the technique recommended by Cooper is Identify Behavioural Variables, that is, he assumes that user research has already been completed and the gathered data have been roughly organized. But the technique does not specifically mention this task. The user survey necessary for eliciting behavioural variables is an implicit activity rather than being stated as the first step of the technique. We came across other similar limitations (up to a total of 11). Table 1 shows the limitations that a software engineer encounters when trying to apply Personas. In each of the activities, we found shortcomings in both the definition of the procedure to be enacted and the formalization of the product resulting from the execution of each activity.

3 Aligning Personas with SE

For each of the limitations found in Table 1, we devised an improvement to be built into Personas. We have incorporated these improvements into a SE version of Personas. The improved Personas avoid the weaknesses encountered by an average software developer unfamiliar with HCI techniques applying the original Personas.

Table 1. Limitations oft he Personas Technique

Activities According to [7]	Limitations with Respect to…	
	How to Perform the Activity	Product to be Output by the Activity
Identify Behavioural Variables	Assumed to have already been completed and that the data gathered have been roughly organized.	No specification of how to record the hypotheses in a proper document.
Map Interview Subjects to Behavioural Variables	No indication of how to output the ranges of the key behavioural variables for mapping.	No formal specification of the content and structure of the product output by this activity.
Identify Significant Behavioural Patterns	No explicit instructions on how to output these patterns.	No specification of any product output by this step.
Synthesize Characteristics and Relevant Goals	No specification of how to synthesize characteristics.	
Check for Completeness and Redundancy	No explicit specification of the procedure to be enacted to carry out this activity.	No mention of the content and structure of the product output by this activity.
Expand the Description of Attributes and Behaviours		Although there is a specification of the content of the product, its structure is unclear.
Designate Persona Types		No formal specification of the content of the product and no specification of the structure.

To be able to build Personas into routine SE developments, it is necessary to define activities and products associated with each activity. We opted to incorporate these improvements into the latest version of the Personas technique published by Cooper et al. [7]. The grounds for this choice were: (i) Cooper made the original proposal; (ii) this proposal was the groundwork for research by other authors; and (iii) this proposal has been successfully used in a number of real projects [8], [11].

Our proposal is composed of a group of activities that, together, lead to the creation of personas. Table 2 sets out these activities with their objectives, techniques and associated products. The new activities or products (not included in any other earlier version of Personas) are highlighted in grey in Table 2. Note that, even for the existing activities, it has been necessary to identify and define both the actual activities and their products using all the existing versions of Personas as sources. Descriptions on how to apply the Personas technique are fuzzy and unordered and results are unrelated [1], [4], [5], [7], [12]. In the new first activity, State Hypotheses for personas, we propose to generate a List of Hypotheses for the Personas that are to be created, as well as developing and holding the interviews with potential users, taking the responses from the Transcribed Interviews to then gather the information required to carry out other activities.

Table 2. Set of Activities Proposed for Personas (new activities are shared grey)

ACTIVITIES		OBJETIVES	TECHNIQUES	PRODUCTS
Activity 1: State Hypotheses	Activity 1.1: Identify Possible Personas	State preliminary hypotheses about the possible personas to be created.	Based on the information gathered from the customer, the nature of the application domain and the organizational documentation gathered at the previous meeting with the customer, developers' state hypotheses for personas. The technique we recommend for this purpose is Brainstorming, followed by a voting round at the end of the session to determine the most creative and feasible hypotheses.	• List of Hypotheses for Personas
	Activity 1.2: Hold Ethnographic Interviews	Based on these hypotheses, investigate possible system users to find out their motivations and behaviours, gathering behavioural data.	The interviews for each hypothesis are conducted based on business domain knowledge and through the proposed ethnographic interviews template.	• Transcribed Interviews
Activity 2: Identify Behavioural Variables	Activity 2.1: Synthesize Interview Responses	Synthesize the responses to all the interviews.	Analyse the results of the survey conducted in activity 1. To do this, process all the responses to the transcribed interview questions using Atlas.ti software (http://www.atlasti.com/) to output the behavioural variables.	• List of Behavioural Variables
	Activity 2.2: List Behavioural Variables	List all behavioural variables. Check identified hypotheses for validity.	Behavioural variables are selected by participative meetings. Then, compare these variables with the personas hypotheses to validate these hypotheses.	• Interview Synthesis
Activity 3: Map Interview Subjects to Behavioural Variables	Activity 3.1: Identify the Ranges of Behavioural Variable Values	For each behavioural variable identify its range of possible values.	At a participatory meeting, analyse the interview synthesis to identify the ranges of each behavioural variable.	• Ranges of Behavioural Variables
	Activity 3.2: Map Interview Subjects to Behavioural Variables	Represent exactly how the multiple subjects are grouped with respect to each of the significant behavioural variables.	Interview subjects are mapped according to the perception of the subjects' observations and the interview responses. To do this, place each of the respondents in different ranges for each of the identified behavioural variables.	• Mapping of Interview Subjects
Activity 4: Identify Significant Behaviour Patterns		Identify particular groups of interview subjects occurring in more than one range or variable.	Examine the mappings of interview subjects from activity 3 and build a table showing the percentage of interview subjects that share each of the behavioural variable range values. The groups with the highest percentages are the significant behaviour patterns. These are the source of the personas, which are given a name and a photograph.	• Percentage Grouping Table • Significant Behaviour Patterns
Activity 5: Synthesize Characteristics and Relevant Goals		Synthesize characteristics and relevant goals. Describe the personas' personalities.	Synthesize the data for each person identified in activity 2, briefly specifying points about the behavioural characteristics identified in the synthesis of the interviews (activity 2).	• Personas Foundation Document
Activity 6: Check for Redundancy and Completeness		Check persona mappings, characteristics and goals.	Check that the important identified aspects are fully defined in the personas created and models built through participatory inspection meetings.	• Validation Document

Table 2. (*continued*)

ACTIVITIES		OBJETIVES	TECHNIQUES	PRODUCTS
Activity 7: Expand the Description of Attributes and Behaviours		Convey the attitudes, personality, needs and problems of the personas to other team members.	Analyse the data collected and the personas grounding document (activity 5) and synthesize the personal profile and a typical day in the life of each persona. For each created persona, write a third-person narrative.	• Narrative
Activity 8: Designate Persona Types	Activity 8.1: Select Representative Personas to Elicit Requirements	Prioritize the created personas to determine which should be the primary design objective, that is, find just one primary persona whose needs and objectives can be completely and positively satisfied by a single interface.	Based on the description of each of the personas types and all the analyses conducted throughout the personas creation process, determine the person types (primary, secondary). Each of the created personas is associated with a personas type.	• Persona Type Association
	Activity 8.2: Enrich the System with Secondary Personas	Determine what secondary persona needs are likely to enrich the system.	Analyse the secondary persona foundation document and narrative and search for functionalities not stated by the primary persona that are useful for the system.	(Software Requirements Specification is enriched)
Activity 9: Build Use Cases		Build annotated use case diagram.	Build the use cases specification taking into account the previously identified behaviour patterns and the information specified in the personas grounding document.	• Annotated Use Case Diagram
		Draft use case specification.		• Use Case Specification
Activity 10: Implement and Evaluate Prototypes	Activity 10.1: Implement Mock-Ups	Build mock-ups.	Based on the use cases developed in the last activity and the previously created personas, build mock-ups.	• Mock-ups
	Activity 10.2: Evaluate Mock-Ups	Validate mock-ups.	At participatory meetings, validate mock-ups.	• Mock-up Evaluation Document

The aim behind the hypotheses for personas is to identify variables that can make a difference between users based on their needs and behaviours. Table 3 shows an example of a List of Hypotheses for Personas. The identification of hypotheses for personas is the first activity to be performed to identify and synthesize personas.

Table 3. Example of List of Hypotheses for Personas for an e-commerce application

Hypothesis	Personas	Explanation
H0	Young People	Young people like technology, are frequent Internet users and shop over the Internet because it is less effort
H1	Professionals, Employees	Shop over the Internet usually for bargains

As part of the activity of Identify Behavioural Variables, we propose a new activity for synthesizing each response to the interviews held in the earlier activity as behavioural variables. Cooper et al. [7] recommend that a list of behavioural variables should be generated from the different aspects of the observed behaviours (Activity 2.2), but this is hard to do from a disaggregated set of information like a set of interviews. For this reason, we add an intermediate step that synthesizes the different interviews into common behaviours.

Behavioural variables are types of behaviour that range across a spectrum [1], [7]. Cooper [7] suggests identifying behavioural variables of the type: activities, attitudes, aptitudes, motivations and abilities. Developers need to elicit the key behavioural variables for every software system as they are domain and task dependent. Often the behavioural variables are implicit in each of the Hypotheses for Personas created in the initial activity where the research was conducted and information gathered. For example, if one of the hypotheses is for a university student, it could be assumed that he will obviously be aged between 18 and 25 years and have some knowledge of computers, although this needs to be double-checked. The implicit variables in this case then are age and computer literacy.

As part of the activity Map Interview Subjects to Behavioural Variables, we propose a new activity for identifying the possible value ranges of each behavioural variable. For example, the possible values for the behavioural variable Frequency of Shopping range from frequent to infrequent. We propose that these variable value ranges should be identified by synthesizing the interview responses. Table 4 illustrates an example of behaviour variables range values.

Table 4. Example of Ranges of Behavioural Variables for an e-commerce application

Behavioural Variables	Scale
Frequency of shopping	Frequent ←→ Infrequent
Desire to shop	Loves to shop ←→ Hates to shop
Motivation to shop	Bargain hunting ←→ Searching for just the right item
Age	From 20 to 30 ←→ Over 61

Interview subjects can be more readily mapped if the value ranges have been defined before the mapping. Cooper [7] describes mapping as positioning each interview subject with respect to one of the behavioural values. The accuracy of this mapping is not critical, but it is important to identify where each interview subject is in relation to the others. There is often no way of measuring the accuracy of this mapping; we have to rely on the perceptiveness of the person doing the mapping. Mapping is done on the basis of the observations of the subjects. Aquino and Leite [2] and Pruitt and Grudin [12] state that the mapping aims to show where each interview subject is positioned with respect to the selected behavioural variables.

The aim of the activity Identify Significant Behaviour Patterns [7] is to detect groupings of particular subjects around multiple ranges or values. A group of subjects clustered around six and eight different variables will represent a significant behaviour pattern that will form the basis of a persona [9]. We propose that this activity output two products: Percentage Grouping Table and Significant Behaviour Patterns. Figure 1 also illustrates an example of Significant Behaviour Patterns.

During the activity of Synthesize Characteristics and Relevant Goals for each identified significant behaviour pattern, we propose that the details of the data gathered from interviews (State Hypotheses Activity) and from the synthesis of the interviews (Identify Behavioural Variables Activity) be synthesized [10]; that is, the environment, a typical work day (or other important period of time), dissatisfactions, and key relationships of potential users with others need to be described. A specification of brief points describing behavioural characteristics will suffice but it needs to include observed possible behaviours. However, an overly fabricated life story, too many quirks, etc., are a distraction and make the personas less credible [10]. Note that we are creating a design tool not an outline of a character for a novel.

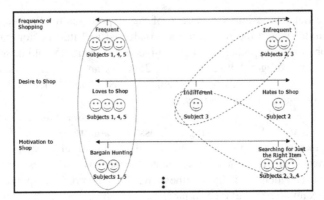

Fig. 1. Fragment of Significant Behaviour Patterns for an e-commerce application

Factual data are the only sound basis for the development and business decisions to be taken by the development team [1], [7]. As a result of this activity, we propose to create, for each identified personas, the Personas Foundation Document. When deciding which characteristics to include in the foundation document, we should think about the type of information that will be useful to the development team. Figure 2 shows the structure and information that we propose for the Personas Foundation Document.

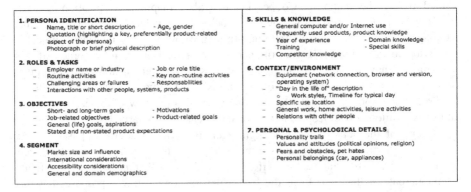

Fig. 2. Proposed Structure for the Personas Foundation Document

The activity Check for Redundancy and Completeness is performed [7] to search for missing information and knowledge. Additional research may be required to discover behaviours that are not to be found in the key behaviour patterns. This would have an impact on all the other activities. At least one significant behaviour should distinguish one persona from any other. We have to assure that, as a whole, the personas are different and complete, and the set of personas is manageable. The proposed output of this activity is to create the Validation Document.

The Personas Foundation Document that we propose states the fundamental nature of complex behaviours but leaves many finer points unmentioned. For this reason, there is an Expand the Description of the Attributes and Behaviours Activity where a narrative is created for each persona [1], [7]. The narrative is a one-page document describing the persona and a typical day in his or her life. The best narrative is one that briefly introduces the persona in terms of his or her job or lifestyle and concisely outlines a day in his or her life, including concerns and interests that have direct implications for the product [1]. The narrative should have a conclusion expressing what the persona is looking for in the product.

We have defined a new activity that links the research done using Personas with the remainder of the development process: Build Use Cases, where use cases are put together based on the Personas Foundation Document and Narrative and the user knowledge acquired throughout all the previous activities. As a result of this activity, we propose that an Annotated Use Case Diagram be built. This diagram is based on the traditional use case diagram, to which we add a brief description of each of the personas involved in the use case. We suggest that the description of the persona contain a brief outline of aspects like the name and type of the persona, as well as an informative note on the use case (Figure 3).

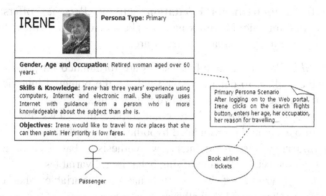

Fig. 3. Annotated Use Case Diagram for the Web Flight Booking System

Finally, we propose a new activity, Implement and Evaluate Prototypes, where mock-ups are built and evaluated. The use cases detailed in the last activity and the knowledge of the user acquired through the other Personas activities need to be taken into account to build the mock-ups. The evaluation that we propose is to be conducted in the actual environment where the potential users routinely carry out their tasks or in convenient meeting rooms where the evaluator can meet with the potential users. We built a tool to help software engineers use the proposed version of Personas. The tool is publicly available at the web site http://arantxa.ii.uam.es/~sacuna/PersonaSE/tool

4   Impact of Incorporating Personas into the Requirements Stage

As Personas synthesizes the data about the users to help identify what the product should do to satisfy the users' needs and profile, the best stage for incorporating this technique into development should be software requirements elicitation. This activity is linked to one or more Personas technique activities (Figure 4). In the following we discuss the impact of Personas on the requirements elicitation phase.

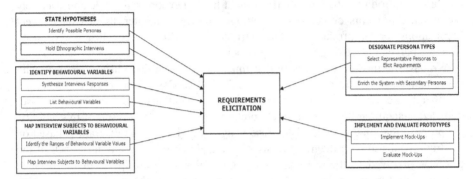

Fig. 4. Integration of the Personas Technique into the Requirements Stage

Regarding the **Requirements Elicitation** activity, Personas offers additional knowledge sources for eliciting information. The Personas activities that have an impact on the requirements elicitation activity are:

- *Identify Possible Personas*: Here hypotheses are formulated for possible personas. These hypotheses help to determine who will be the potential interview subjects. This is the first stage in getting acquainted with the user.
- *Hold Ethnographic Interviews*: Here ethnographic interviews are designed and held taking into account the formulated hypotheses for personas.
- *Synthesize Interview Responses*: Interview synthesis is based on an analysis and synthesis of the interviews for identifying behavioural variables.
- *List Behavioural Variables*: A list of behavioural variables that characterize possible users is taken from the synthesized interviews.
- *Identify the Ranges of Behavioural Variable Values*: The behavioural variable values are obtained by grouping subjects around the behavioural variables. These clusters characterize and provide better knowledge about potential system users.
- *Select Representative Personas to Elicit Requirements*: In this activity, the potential users for routine requirements elicitation are selected.
- *Implement Mock-Ups*: The goal of building mock-ups is to output discussion-based information. Mock-ups explicitly show what the user needs the system to do. The discussion of this mock-up with possible users will end up eliciting additional information.

Summarizing, the use of the Personas technique in a typical requirements stage will have the following benefits:

- Support a proper selection of the user or users that will be the main source of information in the elicitation activity.
- Model the user through the textual representation of their attitudes, needs, jobs, lifestyles, problems, etc.

5   Conclusions

Our research goal was to incorporate HCI knowledge into routine SE practice. Personas is a HCI technique for developing usable interactive applications. We think it is worthwhile to adapt Personas for integration into SE development process. The integration of Personas into the SE requirements stage improves the understanding of what the software product should do and how it should behave. Personas helps to gain a deeper understanding of the users that are to interact with the system and provides support for developing a system that conforms to user characteristics.

Almost all the Personas steps have a series of shortcomings concerning procedure definition and product description. We have modified the HCI Personas technique to comply with the levels of systematization required by SE. We have enriched the SE requirements process by incorporating Personas activities into requirements elicitation stage.

Acknowledgements. This research was supported by Spanish Ministry of Science and Innovation as part of the projects TIN2008-02081 and TIN2008-00555, and by DGUI of the Comunidad de Madrid and UAM as part of GUIDE project: CCG10-UAM/TIC-5772.

References

1. Adlin, T., Pruitt, J.: The Essential Persona Lifecycle: Your Guide to Building and Using Personas. Morgan Kaufmann, Burlington (2010)
2. Aquino, P.T., Leite, L.V.: User Modeling with Personas. In: CLIHC 2005, pp. 277–282. ACM, Cuernavaca (2005)
3. Baecker, H., Carey, C., Mantei, G., Strong, P., Verplank, W.: ACM SIGCHI Curricula for Human-Computer Interaction (1996), http://www2.parc.com/istl/groups/uir/publications/items/UIR-1992-11-ACM.pdf (last updated June 03, 2004)
4. Cooper, A.: The Inmates are Running the Asylum. Macmillan, Indianapolis (1999)
5. Cooper, A., Reimann, R.: About Face 2.0: The Essentials of Interaction Design. Wiley Publishing, Indianapolis (2003)
6. Cooper, A.: The Origin of Personas (2003), http://www.cooper.com/journal/2003/08/the_origin_of_personas.html
7. Cooper, A., Reimann, R., Cronin, D.: About Face 3.0: The Essentials of Interaction Design. Wiley Publishing, Indianapolis (2007)
8. Dong, J., Kelkar, K., Braun, K.: Getting the Most Out of Personas for Product Usability Enhancements. In: UI-HCII, pp. 291–296 (2007)
9. Goodwin, K.: Getting from Research to Personas: Harnessing the Power of Data (2002), http://www.cooper.com/journal/2002/11/getting_from_research_to_perso.html
10. Goodwin, K.: Cooper U Interaction Design Practicum Notes (2002), http://www.cooper.com/services/training/ixd_practicum.html
11. Grudin, J., Pruitt, J.: Personas, Participatory Design and Product Development: An Infrastructure for Engagement. In: Participatory Design Conference (PDC 2002), pp. 144–161. Computer Professionals for Social Responsibility, Sweden (2002)
12. Pruitt, J., Grudin, J.: Personas: Practice and Theory. In: Conference on Designing for User Experience (DUX 2003), pp. 1–15. ACM, New York (2003)

User Attention in Nonlinear Narratives: A Case of Study

Victor Socas-Guerra and Carina S. González-González[*]

Department of System's Engineering and Automatic
University of La Laguna – Tenerife, Spain
cjgonza@ull.es

Abstract. In this paper we present an eye tracking study to evaluate the user experience in an interactive system with a non-linear narrative's structure. New communication formats and exposition freedom are open by user interactions in non-lineal narratives. In order to study the user experience in this kind of systems, we designed, developed and validated an interactive system that break with the classical structure of linear narrative and focus on the non-linearity of the content analysing the perception time and psychological time. However, the user's gaze can be a good indicator of which parts of an interface hold the user's attention. Thus, it is reasonable to assume that the eye-tracking data could be useful to provide information on user experience with the prototype. So, the non-linear narrative structure, the user experience variables and the results of the eye-tracking tests will be discussed in this work.

Keywords: Non-lineal Narrative, Interactive System, Eye-tracking, User Experience.

1   Introduction

Linear stories are written in such a way that the user progresses by reaching predetermined sequential plot points. In contrast, nonlinear narrative, disjointed narrative or disrupted narrative is a narrative technique, wherein events are portrayed out of chronological order. It is often used to mimic the structure and recall of human memory but has been applied for other reasons as well [1].

Nonlinear interactive experiences are translated by the user as a linear; on the other hand, this is a natural human tendency to order on structures already known to explain their experience. Therefore, we can say that the experiences nonlinear become linear user experiences. Then, the problem is not the linear narrative of the presentation or perception, but yes the ideology hidden behind the 'linearity'. Although the contents could be transgressive or anarchic, the form constrains how the public interpret the narrative, in a result that unifies the subject of the narrative. So, linear coherence of the narrative and its conclusion are repressing the subject (viewer) implicitly removing the complexity of its own construction of meaning. Transmitted culturally and validated as a convention, the narrative becomes a model used to interpret experience, and becomes a filter for the external life experience [2].

---

[*] Corresponding author.

F.V. Cipolla-Ficarra et al. (Eds.): CCGIDIS 2011, LNCS 7545, pp. 104–111, 2012.

In our interactive nonlinear narrative there is only one author who lets the user make decisions about their travel narrative. This requires constant activity that somehow approximates the author-user roles without confusing, because even though the links can be chosen freely, all have been designed and introduced previously by an author who does not lose control of the narrative. Here, the user does not build; decide on what has been built. This interactive system of nonlinear narrative is known as exploratory hyper-fiction.

On the other hand, the design of the interfaces in nonlinear narrative systems is often quite rudimentary or too complicated and distracting from the main content with peripheral information. This may be due mostly to the main content is still written in linear fashion, i.e. with a structure and characters story-lines.

The most common problem is the end user feeling of having been involved in a classical linear narrative experience (Aristotelian structure), the opposite of what we want, as our content break with the classical structure of linear narrative and focus on the non-linearity of the content, analysing the perception time and psychological time. Moreover, previous studies [3] showed that a user's gaze can be a good indicator of which parts of an interface hold the user's attention. Thus, it is reasonable to assume that the eye-tracking data could be useful to provide information on user experience with the prototype.

The lack of user studies to this type of systems hamper this research, so we have created a prototype non-linear narrative with three different interfaces user studies to address this type of system. In particular, in this paper we describe our inclusion of eye-tracking information to track exploration behaviour in non-linear narratives.

2 Eye-Tracking Background

Retrospective analysis of eye movement data has been studied to evaluate usability issues and understand human performance [4]. For instance, Schiessl *et al.* [5] used an eye-tracker to investigate gender differences in attention behaviour for textual *vs.* pictorial stimuli on websites. An interesting outcome was that, when the participants were asked where in the interface they thought they looked, their perceptions often differed from reality, showing that accurate attention patterns could only be found with an eye-tracker. In [6], offline processing of eye-tracking data was used to improve the efficient generation of non-photo-realistic images. Users' eye fixations were analyzed to determine which parts of given pictures users found to be most meaningful, and the findings were used to design algorithms that draw the most "important" parts of the picture first.

There has also been fairly extensive research in using eye gaze as an alternative form of input to allow a user to explicitly operate an interface. In [7], Jakob explores issues surrounding the real-time processing of eye data such as efficient noise reduction and the organization of gaze information into tokens from which relevant data may be extracted. He then discusses the potential of eye-tracking as a tool in several forms of interface manipulation, including object selection/movement, scrolling text, and navigating menus.

A parallel research stream has used eye-tracking data on-line for real-time interaction adaptation. Some of this work uses gaze tracking to assess user task performance. In [8], Iqbal and Bailey use gaze-tracking to determine which type of task the user is performing (i.e., reading email vs. reading a web page), with the goal of devising an attention manager that balances the user's need for minimal disruption with an application's need to deliver necessary information. There has also been research on using gaze information for real-time adaptation to user *mental states* such as interest or problem-solving strategies. In [9], Starker and Bolt describe a system that uses an eye-tracker to determine which part of a graphical interface a user is interested in, and then provides more information about this area via visual zooming or synthesized speech.

The study described in this paper contributes to the above body of work by providing initial indications to evaluate the user experience in interactive non-lineal narratives [10].

3   Study Design

Our research has focused on creating and evaluating the interactive user experience in a non-linear narrative. So we've created three prototypes developing the concept of gender violence. To design the interfaces of the system we followed the user-centred design (UCD) following the goals of: a) developing a usable interface to the very low level of distraction, b) using as interaction style the direct manipulation, c) adapting the content to the concepts to be treated, in this case gender violence, d) reinforcing concepts with representative images and videos, and finally, e) creating a content architecture that enhances the self narrative, trough images, video and stories embedded.

3.1   Prototype Design

The prototype of non-linear narrative (PNL) is composed of four video narratives related in function of user decisions (Figure 1). The relation among narratives are temporal and is conditioned by the decisions that the user takes when pass from the one narrative to other. However, the relation is composed by a set of facts or showed incidents, transitions elements, chronological organization of the message, perception time and psychological time.

Narrative	Content	D	Video
01	Gender Violence	6′	

Fig. 1. Type of contents

Narrative	Content	D	Video
02	Stereotype	6′	
03	Landscape	6′	
04	Water Lilies,	6′	

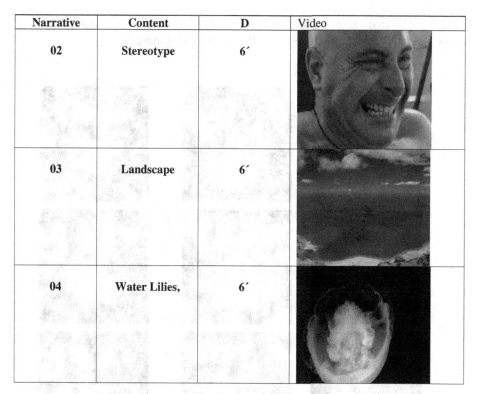

Fig. 1. (*continued*)

4   Validation

In order to analyse the user experience using the different interfaces of our non-linear narrative prototype we used several techniques, such as: a) cognitive walk-through, b) inquiries, c) thinking aloud and, d) eye tracking. For the test sessions, we have selected five experts with large experience in the fields of technology, arts, video games, communication.

During the sessions, at first we have explained to the experts the mechanic of the system and then, the experts has to interact with the system thinking aloud during all session. However, we have monitored the user gaze with eye tracker and recorded in video for a post data analysis. Moreover, after the interaction with the system, the experts completed a test taking into account the perception time and the invasive constraints of interfaces.

In particular, to study the human factor in an interactive user experience related with the type of interactive narrative presented, we analysed the followed parameters: a) perception time, b) physiological time and c) invasive constraints of interfaces.

On the eye-tracking test we have studied the followed parameters:

1. Media duration of visual fixation
2. Time of first visual fixation
3. Media of clicks
4. Total visual fixation

After the data analysis of the sessions with the experts we obtained a comparative of results among the three interfaces of the PNL prototype (Figure 2):

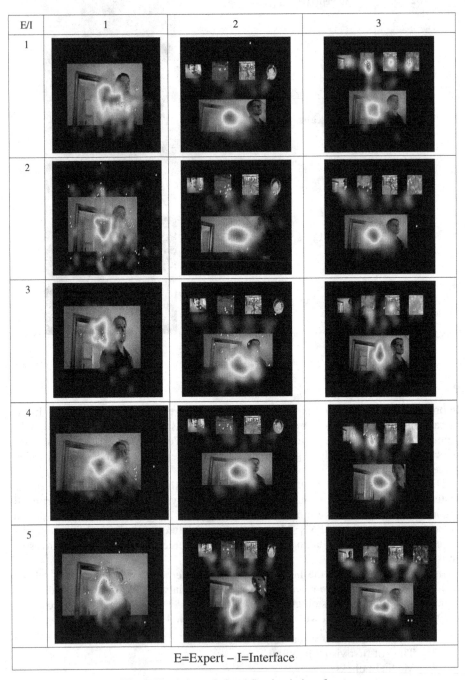

Fig. 2. Total time of visual fixation in interfaces

The two interfaces with buttons presents important differences in the user attention as we can observe in Figure 3:

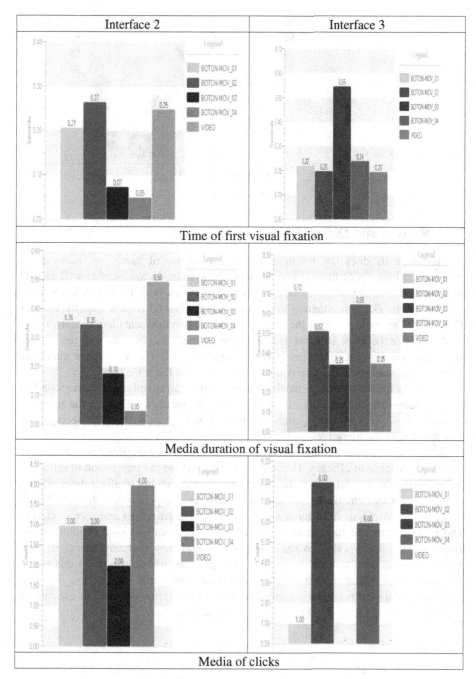

Fig. 3. Comparative results of parameters

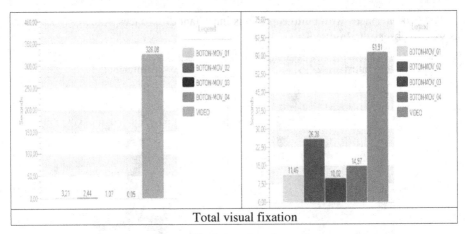

Total visual fixation

Fig. 3. (*continued*)

5   Results and Discussions

The interface 01 does not produce an active response of user. It is necessary a previous explanation of how to interact with the system. In the interfaces 02 and 03 we observed that the most relevant difference between both interfaces is the total visual fixation. The user attention in the interface number 03 is more than the number 02 and 01. The reason is than the buttons are videos and presents movements. Other result of this experience has that users interpreted the video-buttons with the options to the narrative as part of the narrative. These results allow us to propose interfaces composed by various interactive non-linear narratives at the same time.

The video format invites to receive passively the narrative but the background of the user seems to influence the interaction with the narrative. Thus, in the interface 01, only the expert in videogames understood immediately that the necessity of interaction with the narrative.

The key to nonlinear narrative is variability and the user experience is enhanced by variety and a sense of efficacy. Users are at least provided the impression of influence in the world that they interact. When you give users the ability to affect the narrative, you produce more emotional investment in their user experience. Future work will focus on the development of more non-linear narrative structures and user models to help us to understand their emotions and experience with this kind of interactions. Moreover, we are working in the design of several new narrative pieces to treat physiological or post-traumatic disorders, like phobias among others. In this sense, the non-intrusive and non-verbal measurement instrument, as an eye tracking hardware and a statistical system, could help us to determine the level of excitement to an image and if the emotion is of a pleasant or unpleasant.

References

1. Szilas, N.: Structural Models for Interactive Drama. In: The proceedings of the 2nd International Conference on Computational Semiotics for Games and New Media, Augsburg, Germany (September 2002)
2. Skov, M.B., Borgh Andersen, P.: Designing Interactive Narratives. In: Proc. of Computational Semiotics for Games and New Media, Amsterdam (September 2001)
3. Monty, R.A., Senders, J.W. (eds.): Eye Movements and Psychological Processes. Lawrence Erlbaum Associates, Hillsdale (1976)
4. Conati, C., Merten, C.: Eye-Tracking for User Modelling in Exploratory Learning Environments: an Empirical Evaluation. Knowledge Based Systems, vol. 20(6). Elsevier Science Publishers B. V., Amsterdam (2007)
5. Schiessl, M., Duda, S., Tholke, A., Fischer, R.: Eye Tracking and Its Application in Usability and Media Research. Sonderheft: Blickbewegung in MMI-Interaktiv Journal 6 (2003)
6. Decarlo, D., Santella, A.: Stylization and Abstraction of Photographs. In: 29th Annual Conference on Computer Graphics and Interactive Techniques, pp. 769–776 (2002)
7. Jakob, R.: The Use of Eye Movements in Human-Computer Interaction Techniques: What You Look at Is What You Get, pp. 65–83 (1998)
8. Iqbal, S.T., Bailey, B.P.: Using Eye Gaze Patterns to Identify User Tasks. The Grace Hopper Celebration of Women in Computing (2004)
9. Starker, I., Bolt, R.A.: A Gaze-Responsive Self- Disclosing Display. In: CHI: Human Factors in Computing Systems (1990)
10. Laurillard, D., Stratfold, M., Luckin, R., Plowman, L., Taylor, J.: Affordances for Learning in a Non-Linear Narrative Medium. Journal of Interactive Media in Education (2000)

Cloud Technology: The Driving Force of Change in the Business Environment

Beatriz Sainz de Abajo[1], Javier Sánchez González[1],
Francisco Javier Burón Fernández[2], Enrique García Salcines[2],
Miguel López Coronado[1], and Carlos de Castro Lozano[2]

[1] Telecommunications Technical School (ETSIT), University of Valladolid,
Campus Miguel Delibes, Paseo de Belén nº 15, 47011 Valladolid, Spain
{beasai,miglop}@tel.uva.es, jsanchez_43@hotmail.com
[2] EATCO Research Group, University of Cordoba
Edificio Leonardo da Vinci, Campus de Rabanales, 14071 Córdoba, Spain
{egsalcines,jburon,malcaloc}@uco.es

Abstract. A series of changes relating to digital environments and the Internet are taking place. Most of these changes are due to the emergence of the concept of Cloud. This will result in a series of advantages for the users, since they will be able to use the data and different software tools available on the Internet. This article begins by introducing the reader to the environment surrounding the Cloud Technology. The background and system architecture will be discussed. Eucalyptus, OpenNebula and Nimbus, three of the main open source software platforms used in Cloud Computing, will also be analyzed. Finally, an analysis about how Cloud Technology may produce changes at the social, personal and business level is put forward. This article intends to provide the reader with an idea about the way in which, thanks to the use and development of Cloud Technology, a notable change in information technology is produced.

Keywords: Cloud Technology, Grid Computing, Outsourcing, Small and Medium Enterprise (SME), Virtualization.

1 Introduction

Nowadays, we have a lot of ways to communicate with our family, friends, couple and/or colleagues. Think about a normal day. You may want to send an e-mail to your mother or father, you may be chatting with your friends in a café, uploading photos of your last holidays to Facebook or even looking up the address of your best friend in Gmail. Now we can do all these things whenever and wherever we want, by using cutting-edge mobile devices.

You may not realize, but you could be up in the clouds, the most suitable word in this context. In fact, you may be using a new information processing paradigm without even knowing it. Floating in a virtual way, every one of us is surfing in a space where anything we want is remotely processed, so we can see the answers to our search in the screens of our personal communication devices. On the other hand, we have to take into account the economic implications at the global level of these

F.V. Cipolla-Ficarra et al. (Eds.): CCGIDIS 2011, LNCS 7545, pp. 112–121, 2012.

Internet improvements and advances. There are many reasons why such a change should be promoted. This revolution associated to Cloud Computing sustains itself with the idea that its implementation facilitates the democratization related to the access to a great amount of advanced services which until recently were a luxury for the most of the companies, either because of their cost or because of their through-put times, increasing by their implementation the global agility and flexibility of the answers associated with this environment. All this is very important in a moment like the current one, marked by the cuts and the crisis in many countries. Another factor which encourages companies to try Cloud Computer is the possibility to administrate remote offices easily, through an off-site medium. The main European economies will also be favored by the use of Cloud Technology, earning hundreds of billions Euro, mainly due to the adoption of the hybrid and private models. Currently, the technology is able to face the new challenge consisting of placing the information on the Internet, taking advantage of the ubiquity and the collaborative work and thus creating a tool which allows to carry out the work in a more efficient way. Some reasons have already been presented, but other reasons relating to this issue of change may be looked up in the references [1], [2], [3], [4] and [5]. In order for Cloud Technology to be successful, it has to be simple and easy to use. Moreover, a price model must be created. Through the implementation of Cloud Technology, the general expenses of support and maintenance will be drastically reduced, as in the Cloud Technology environment not all the users must have hardware, computers, routers, servers, etc., since Cloud's users share those things (this is called "virtual possession"). This already existed a long time before the "Cloud Technology age", c.f. "famous diskless Oracle station in middle 90ties or even shared printer Spooler". The main difference is in the cloud, we will never know where our software is executed. In short, the user will only have to pay for the programmes or services which he uses. This concept is called "Pay-as-you-use" model, particularly recommended for small and medium enterprises (SME) [6]. Internet has led to the globalization of products and services and has placed itself as the ideal platform for the development of SMEs [7]. This piece of work aims at putting forward a general description of the Cloud Technology, as well as explaining its advantages, components, types and notable applications. We will discuss the fundamentals of Cloud Technology as compared to Grid environment, which are currently used. There will also be a section for conclusions and discussion about the future of Cloud Technology.

2   Background

Some ideas constitute the main pillars of Cloud Technology. The cloud is based on the idea that the resources can be shared among the users but they must be managed by other people. In order to achieve this aim, it is necessary to resort to some techniques such as the automation and virtualization. According to this idea, the solution reached must be flexible to the dynamic changes in accordance with the requests from a company. Moreover, one of the main features of the Cloud

Technology is that there should be an interaction among systems, data and users in such a way that "the required interaction with the underlying layers of the whole set of technological solutions is reduced to a minimum" [8].

Cloud Technology offers some advantages which will be hardly achieved with other solutions. One of these advantages is the greater amount of data which can be stored at a lower price. Moreover, since less hardware for each specific user is needed, because it is shared by a lot of them, Cloud Technology reduces the costs associated with the maintenance of all the updated devices. This solution also provides users with a greater mobility. This could be used to promote outsourcing businesses or the differentiation in the infrastructure's level of service. The main disadvantage is that the innovation could be challenged due to the centralization process required by Cloud Technology, which could result in the creation of long-lasting normalized systems [9]. Cloud Technology users or commercial enterprises become more flexible with the use of this solution. The cloud raises hopes for globalization, since its scalability makes it ideal for providing services to billions of users in the whole world.

On the other hand, one could think that the use of this system is less harmful to the environment, since it limits the energy consumption and/or CO_2 emissions. But actually, some calculations must be provided – either in the mobile or in some place of the cloud. The energy required is the same in both cases. This is the same situation than that of the electric car – this is not a real "environmentally friendly" solution, since in order to obtain the energy for your car you have to produce it from, for example, oil or fuel. The only difference is that CO_2 is produced in another place, not close to me. This may be a real reason, but not the "lower emission".

3   Layers of Cloud Technology Architecture

Virtualization and management are supported by the different levels of the Cloud Technology Stack, as shown in figure 1 [10]:

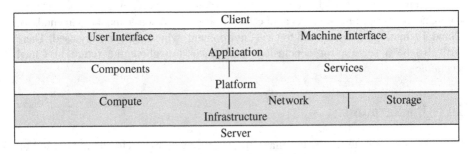

Fig. 1. Cloud Technology Stack

Each architecture's layer is explained:

3.1   SaaS

When you pay for software services through the Internet, you normally use platform types that you do not specifically possess, so you have to pay for using them. You do not program or develop anything, but in some cases, you can personalize your application software. We can see here the features of the Cloud price model, you only pay for what you use. There is a fact which shows the spirit of Cloud, the reason why other IaaS (Infrastructure as a Service) or PaaS (Platform as a Service) providers support the operations of some SaaS (Software as a Service) suppliers. Some examples of services implemented through this type of service model are email or business software, etc. Sometimes, a licence is used, in other cases a "free-of-charge" methodology is followed. Nowadays, the main Cloud software services use Google Apps (including Gmail) and Salesforce CMR (provided by Salesforce.com). In order to handle the application, the user does not need to install any code in their computer, since it may be used from a web browser, such as Gmail from Google. You only have to observe figure 2 [1]:

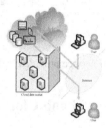

Fig. 2. Software Service provided by the Cloud (SaaS)

3.2   PaaS

When a provider supplies the hardware, as if it was an IaaS, and he also adds some application software, this provider is called PaaS. The software developed through a PaaS user can be consulted by executing the Cloud data centre. The remote access to the server entails that the developer might not know its location, since he only uses the server resources. This results in reduced implementation and development time, as well as reduced costs. PaaS offers all the required possibilities for supporting the full lifecycle of creation and publication of web applications and services. We will see below figure 3 [1]:

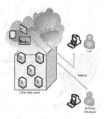

Fig. 3. Platform Service provided by the Cloud (PaaS)

3.3   IaaS

Traditional hosting will progress to IaaS, where in a long-term commitment it will allow users to access their resources on demand. The difference between IaaS and PaaS services is that, in the case of IaaS, its provider carries out very little amounts of management of the services, letting users deploy and manage the software services as they please, as if it were their own data centre. After entering the web page of the Cloud service provider, (1) as in Figure 4 [1], the user accesses and enters by defining the compulsory characteristics of the computer, such as memory and HDD capacity, CPU and operating system type, etc (2). When the Cloud centre receives the request, such centre prepares a "virtual" computer in the data centre by using the user's requirements. Now the user can treat it like if it were an old mini-mainframe system, communicating only through the Internet.

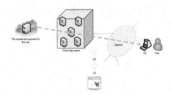

Fig. 4. Infrastructure Service provided by the Cloud (IaaS)

4   Comparison between Grid and Cloud Technology

There exists some resemblance among the above issues. Both of them are aimed at joining to create the Next Generation Network (NGN). Moreover, they will be able to develop a reciprocal effect taking advantage of NGN evolution capacities. To reach this objective, Grid and Cloud Technology do not need to be managed by telecommunication operators to improve the networks of the companies which need a great amount of processed data. The fact that they were controlled by telecommunications operators would mean the end of this business. Operators, particularly telecommunications companies, must act in a transparent way as network providers, not as service providers. Grid and Cloud technologies will also take advantage from each other. Cloud-based systems may be at the same time Grid-based and vice versa (but it is more difficult to imagine why).

As regards what we stated before, on the one hand it would be possible to share resources in a distributive way, or to integrate normalized interfaces and, on the other hand, the virtualization layer may be improved. As regards the differences between them, a small summary is worth doing. Despite the fact that the interfaces which use the web paradigm are typical of Cloud, the objective of Grid is to implement collaboration tools to favour "complex resource linking", not for "resource sharing"; i.e. the main difference is that Grid is designed for sharing complex services with different administrative domains, whereas Cloud shows more basic resources and from a sole domain. This discrepancy in the orientation of both technologies entails a difference in the management complexity. Grid has quite a considerable additional complexity, which is mainly related to the geographic distribution of the resources and to the participation of multiple administrative domains. Cloud-based computing does correspond, so far, to the notion of on-demand computing. In this model, "CPU hours" supplied by a provider, generally commercial, are accessed and invoiced according to consumption and quality. By contrast, Grid-computing model has some limitations which restrict the applications which can take advantage of it. Precisely, elasticity is one of the characteristics of on-demand computing systems, which offers an efficient way to use more or less resources depending on the applications needs. For instance, Cloud-based computing allows to use more resources if there is a peak in a service's demand and turn off resources which are not being used. Consequently, the cost of migrating a job in Grid is, generally, high. This is another reason for improving the processes of resource planning and assignment. All things considered, of all the differences mentioned between Cloud and Grid we have to highlight, due to its great importance, those relating to the different computing types, resource distribution, distributed applications (really distributed, i.e., each sub-process in a different location), etc. Despite the fact that Cloud is the evolution of Grid, there are still some areas where Grid is more advanced. This can be specially seen with regard to data privacy and security, since in the Cloud environment we must take into account that the user's information will always be exposed to more danger than if it was stored in a third server. However, most clients do not know the conditions under which they access data or their storage method [11] [12].

5   Cloud Computing Software Platforms Based on an Open Source

The main three ones are Eucalyptus, OpenNebula and Nimbus. The main function of all of them is to manage the provision of virtual machines with the purpose of facilitating a Cloud in the shape of Infrastructure as a Service. In some cases, such as an organization with many users, it can make more economic sense for that enterprise to buy hardware instead of creating its private cloud. Here Eucaplytus, OpenNebula and Nimbus come on stage, since they allow such an organization to create a private machine group as its own cloud.

The following figure shows the steps to analyze a virtual machine with an Eucalyptus configuration, which will be explained below [13]:

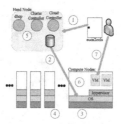

Fig. 5. Eucalyptus

1) The user uses euca2ools, which is a programme similar to Amazon EC2 front-end programmes to request a virtual machine. 2) The template of the disk image virtual machine is inserted in a compute node. 3) Such a disk image is adjusted to the appropriate size and packing to be used by the hypervisor in the compute node. 4) The compute node establishes the network bridge to provide a virtual NIC with a virtual MAC. 5) In the main node, the DHCP is configured with the MAC/IP pair. 6) The virtual machine is generated in the VMM (Virtual Machine Monitor). 7) The user can now use SSH directly in the virtual machine.

OpenNebula is mainly characterised by providing the final users with high levels of personalization and centralization. We will discuss now the steps which constitute the analysis of a virtual machine under this environment. 1) A user uses SSH to access the head node. 2) The user uses the onevm command to request a virtual machine. 3) The template of the disk image virtual machine is copied and a copy is adapted to the right configuration and size within the NFS directory in the head node (catalogued as nfsd). 4) The oned process, also placed at the head node, uses SSH to access the compute node. 5) The compute node sets the network bridge to provide a virtual NIC with a virtual MAC. 6) The files needed by VMM in the compute node will be dragged to the compute node through the NFS. 7) The virtual machine is generated in VMM. 8) The user can now use SSH directly in the virtual machine. *) Generally, the DHCP server is managed independently from the OpenNebula configuration. The following figure is clear enough to explain this [13]:

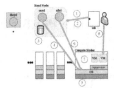

Fig. 6. OpenNebula

The Nimbus project was explicitly announced as a "science" Cloud solution. In its new version, it uses Cumulus, a system which, like Eucalyptus' Walrus, is compatible with S3. It shares with OpenNebula the feature that both of them have a high personalizable character. Figure 7 shows the steps to analyze a virtual machine with a Nimbus configuration, which are discussed below:

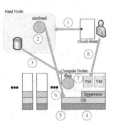

Fig. 7. Nimbus

1) A user uses a cloud-client to request a virtual machine. 2) Nimbus uses SSH in the compute node. 3) The template of the disk image virtual machine is inserted in the compute node (in Nimbus more recent versions this will be done by using a distributed storage similar to S3 and Walrus). 4) In the compute node, the disk image is adapted to the right size and it is configured. 5) The compute node establishes a network bridge to provide a virtual NIC with a virtual MAC. 6) A DHCP server in the compute node is configured with the MAC/IP pair. 7) The virtual machine is generated in VMM. 8) The user can now use SSH directly in the virtual machine.

6   Conclusions

The concept of Cloud Computing itself is not such a novel one. On the other hand, some improvements will be made so that the servers can deal with the requests of more concurrent users, the deployment of more access networks at higher speed might be promoted if there is enough demand, etc. The change towards virtualization, not at the technological level, but at the level of user experience and of being able of accessing your documents from any terminal is also important. Therefore, the technological innovation is questionable, but the innovation on terms of experience and usability is not questionable thanks to the advance of the network technology and telecommunication systems (broadband and mobility). All this suggests that in the near future the convergence among Grid, Cloud and NGN is more than necessary. The fact that the telecommunication operators consider that the new tendencies are based on the convergence of fixed and mobile data services in NGN, since each type of service usually uses its own platform with a minimum interoperability, is striking [14]. The governments of several countries could be those which benefited most from the emergence of Cloud Technology. Cloud Technology itself cannot reduce the administration and computing problems which may arise, what it can certainly do is to reduce the possible obstacles by eliminating delays and reducing costs. It is a type of technology adequate for government users due to, among other things, its reliability, lower maintenance cost, flexibility, etc [15]. This technology can also be analyzed from different points of view in order to understand its worldwide impact, in particular, we will do it from the social, sector business and personal perspective. As far as the changes linked to the first of them are concerned, we must say that the decrease of the social burden is linked to the work reduction, in order to build appropriate computing environments, as well as supplying several services based on what is known as Information and Communication Technologies (ICT). As regards the possible changes in the sector business the reduction of development burden associated with new products and services which are beginning to appear stands out, materializing in aspects such as costs and time. With regard to personal changes which should occur, we must mention that the Cloud will provide the user with more business opportunities, as well as learning and employment chances [1].

With regard to future opportunities linked to the three software platforms analyzed in the present document, i.e. Eucalyptus, OpenNebula and Nimbus, a series of conclusions classified by two fundamental aspects (Scheduling and Networking) will be discussed here. As far as Scheduling is concerned, an area of knowledge is that connected to virtual machines. In this environment, in the default configurations of OpenNebula and Eucalyptus, no real programming practice is carried out, with regard to negotiation of priority for the processors. Instead, if the resources for a requested virtual machine are available, they are assigned, otherwise they are not. Nimbus, for its part, restricts the users in the number and size of the machines they can create. We must also say that a simple front-end performing the same function could easily be added to Eucalyptus and OpenNebula. The mechanism for programming a private Cloud is the affirmative or negative decision for a particular requested renting. Since the decision has to be made at the moment of the request without taking into account future requests, what we said above results in the existence of an online algorithm problem. Then, the following question comes up: Which online algorithm can plan the requests relating to the virtual machine resources, lacking the economic aspect, in such a way that the computing resources are available for high priority users without unnecessarily letting the resources inactive? This becomes a discussion issue in which the users hope to have access to the private Cloud. Once the first aspect analyzed, Scheduling, we must tackle the second one, Networking. In this context, the term "virtual networking" of the virtual machines is often used. Nimbus, particularly, has a great interest in the groups of virtual machines, completed with a virtual network among them. This idea underlies in the concept of clouds offering renting to virtual machines, instead of the task planning. In the practice, the weaker aspects, in all the cases, of those programmes' assembly is the configuration of the Cloud Controller to work with different network parameters. In short, each of the Clouds is responsible for assigning IP addresses slightly different from the virtual machines. The problems which may arise if the network administrator and the Cloud administrator are not the same person are easy to see. As far as Eucalyptus is concerned, if the routers are configured to filter traffic which is not for certain IP addresses, the routing tables must be coordinated with the Eucalyptus IP/MAC lists. For its part, in OpenNebula, the administrator must have the possibility of managing its own DHCP server and know which MAC and IP address combination will not conflict with the rest of the network. The problem of filtering which occurred in Nimbus also appears in Eucalyptus, as well as different issues which may arise if the filtered MAC address is used. To sum up, Eucalyptus, OpenNebula and Nimbus have the big problem of the existence of network conflicts if each of them is not the only element within their own subnetworks. To solve this problem, if it occurs at the business level, either only the Cloud sub-networks assigned for that shall be used, either the Cloud Controller programs should be made more flexible, both as regards virtual networks and external network administration [13].

References

1. Kurokawa, T., Hidaka, K.: Promises of Cloud Computing: Underlying Technology That Supports Transformation From Possession to Utilization. Science and Technology Trends-Quarterly Review 37, 40–52 (2010)

2. What cloud computing really means. InfoWorld,
http://www.infoworld.com/d/cloud-computing/what-cloud-computing-really-means-031

3. Full Interview: AT&T's Joe Weinman. Green Telecom Live,
http://www.greentelecomlive.com/2009/03/16/full-interview-atts-joe-weinman/

4. Rodriguez Martinez, M., Seguel, J., Greer, M.: Open Source Cloud Computing Tools: A Case Study with a Weather Application. In: Proceedings of IEEE 3rd International Conference on Cloud Computing (CLOUD), Miami, pp. 443–449 (2010)

5. Wei, G., Athanasios, V., Zheng, Y., Xiong, N.: A game-theoretic method of fair resource allocation for cloud computing services. The Journal of Supercomputing 54(2), 252–269 (2010)

6. National Public Radio, http://www.npr.org/templates/story/story.php?storyId=102453091

7. Sainz de Abajo, B., de la Torre Diez, I., Lopez-Coronado, M.: Analysis of benefits and risks of e-commerce. Practical study of Spanish SME. In: Portela, I.M., Cruz-Cunha, M.M. (eds.) Information Communication Technology Law, Protection and Access Rights: Global Approaches and Issues, pp. 214–239 (2010)

8. Cloud Computing: Get Your Head in the Clouds. Production Scale,
http://www.productionscale.com/home/2008/4/24/cloud-computing-get-your-head-in-the-clouds.html

9. Opinion: No End in Sight. Computerworld, http://www.computerworld.com/managementtopics/management/story/0,10801,101705,00.html

10. Bhardwaj, S., Jain, L., Jain, S.: Cloud computing: A study of infrastructure as a service (IaaS). International Journal of Engineering and Information Technology 2(1), 60–63 (2010)

11. Kovacikova, T.: Grid and Cloud Computing Integration with NGN. In: Proceedings of the 13th WSEAS International Conference on Communications, pp. 88–94 (2009)

12. Cloud Computing: Need of the hour, http://www.rimtengg.com/iscet/proceedings/pdfs/advcomp/44.pdf

13. Sempolinski, P., Thain, D.: An Comparison and Critique of Eucalyptus, OpenNebula and Nimbus. In: IEEE Second International Conference on Cloud Computing Technology and Science, pp. 417–426 (2010)

14. Rings, T., Caryer, G., Gallop, J., Grabowski, J., Kovacikova, T., Schulz, S., Stokes-Rees, I.: Grid and Cloud Computing: Opportunities for Integration with the Next Generation Network. Journal of Grid Computing 7(3), 375–393 (2009)

15. Nelson, M.R.: The Cloud, the Crowd, and Public Policy. Issues in Science & Technology 25(4), 71–76 (2009)

Ubiquitous TV with HTML5

Francisco Javier Burón Fernández[1], Rafael Mena[1], Beatriz Sainz de Abajo[2],
Enrique García Salcines[1], and Carlos de Castro Lozano[1]

[1] EATCO Research Group, University of Cordoba,
Edificio Leonardo da Vinci, Campus de Rabanales, 14071 Córdoba, Spain
{egsalcines,jburon,malcaloc}@uco.es
[2] Telecommunications Technical School (ETSIT), University of Valladolid,
Campus Miguel Delibes, Paseo de Belén nº 15, 47011 Valladolid, Spain
beasai@tel.uva.es

Abstract. The wide adoption of small and powerful mobile computers, such as smart phones and tablets, has raised the opportunity to employ them in multi-user and multi-device iTV scenarios. In particular, the standardization of HTML5 and the increase of cloud services have made the web browser a suitable tool for managing multimedia content and the user interface, in order to provide seamless session mobility among devices, such as smart phones, tablets and TV screens. In this paper we present architecture and a prototype that let people transfer instantaneously the video they are watching between web devices. This architecture is based on two pillars: Websockets, a new HTML5 feature, and Internet TV (Youtube, Yahoo Video, Vimeo, etc.). We demonstrate the flexibility of the proposed architecture in a prototype that employs the Youtube API and that facilitates seamless session mobility in a ubiquitous TV scenario. This flexible experimental set-up let us test several hypotheses, such as user attention and user behavior, in the presence of multiple users and multiple videos on personal and shared screens.

Keywords: iTV, HTML5, Websockets.

1   Introduction

Since the advent of the PDAs there have been some studies to replace the remote control in the interaction with interactive television. One of the most influential research for this work is the Robertson one (1996), which proposed a prototype for real estate searching by a PDA bidirectionally communicated via infrared with interactive television. The author proposes a design guide remarking the importance of distributing information through appropriate devices. So the right information for display on PDA's is text and some icons, but television is suitable for displaying large images, video or audio. So the nature and quantity of information determines how to display and on which device. This research also gives priority to increase a synchronized cooperation between both devices.

By now user interface systems consider a clear distinction between the input and the output devices. Indeed, the user interface systems in desktop computers, TVs,

F.V. Cipolla-Ficarra et al. (Eds.): CCGIDIS 2011, LNCS 7545, pp. 122–126, 2012.
© Springer-Verlag Berlin Heidelberg 2012

telephones, have usually distinguished between the input and the output devices. Smart phones and tablets are devices that don't consider this distinction. Moreover, the plentitude of devices enable the creation of ubiquitous computing scenarios, where the user can interact with two of more devices. Then, one significant research issue is to balance the visual interface system between two devices with output abilities.

The remote control has been the most common way to interact with iTV. Moreover, some released products as RedEye that let the user interacts with TV through a second screen to do some basic operations of content controlling, however, it works only like Wifi to Infrared traductor in different devices. However, the popularity of mobile computers such as smart phones and tablets allow us to leverage the established way of interaction. A second screen could give the user more information and the possibility to interact controlling, enriching or sharing the content (Cesar et al. 2009, Cesar 2008). In this work, the researchers examine alternative scenarios for controlling the content in a dual screen set-up.

2   System Architecture

In our research, we are exploring alternative multi-device visual interface configurations in the context of a leisure environment and for entertainment applications. For this purpose, we have developed a flexible experimental set-up, which we plan to employ in several user evaluations. The latter are focused on the actual user behavior in the face of important parameters, such as attention, engagement, and enjoyment.

The system architecture for the experimental set-up consists of: 1) A Tv connected to a Laptop, 2) Apache/PHP Server, 3) An Ipad and Iphone, 4) A Local Area Network, 5) An Apple Remote connected to the TV using Infrared. In Figure 2 a simplified draw of the system arcuitecture, in order to be well understood, can be observed. Firstly it is necessary to remark that the novelty of this architecture is the use of a technology drafted in HTML5 called WebSockets. The use of this technology let us connect bidirectionally two browsers. Thanks to this characteristic we convert an Ipad or any device with a WebSockets supported browser in a TV remote controller. For this several webs (depending on the scenario) have been developed. From these webs the user will be able to control other Webs that represent the TV.

This work is focused on the secondary-screen as a control device for TV content. Previous research has regarded the secondary-screen as an editing and a sharing interface, but has neglected the control aspect. In particular, we are seeking to understand the balance between the shared and the personal screen during alternative TV-control scenarios that regard the secondary-screen as a: 1) simple remote control, 2) related information display, 3) mirror of the same TV content.

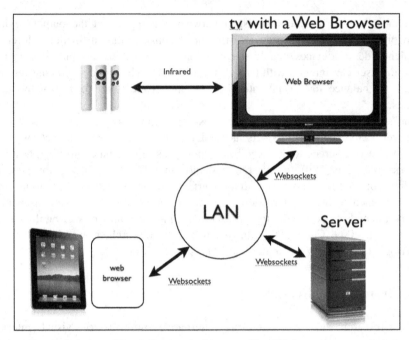

Fig. 1. System Architecture Simplified

3   Ongoing Research

For our research we consider the following situation: Peter is watching a list of short sailing videos and he wants to control the video content playing, pausing and stopping the video, pass to the next and the previous video and see more information about the video including the next video. It is worth highlighting that the proposed functionality is a subset of that provided by the API of YouTube, which is a rather diverse and growing pool of video content. Is necessary to remark that the researchers want to evaluate interaction concepts on iTV. For this very simple actions will take in part in these prototypes to come up with conclusion for the design of coupled display interfaces in general in a leisure environment.

So far we have developed four scenarios of iTV interaction:

1. To Interact with iTV using a remote control: In this case, user interacts with iTV using remote controller. To control the content there is a play/pause button and two arrows, right and left, to select the next or the previous video. The Menu button will be used to show the information related to the video and the next video on the list.
2. To interact with iTV using a tablet as remote controller: In this case, all the overlay information shown in the first scenario is displayed in the tablet cleaning the first screen of interactive information so it wouldn't disturb other users.

3. To interact with iTV using a tablet as remote controller: In this case, all the overlay information is displayed in the TV.
4. iTV inside the tablet and a screen shared: This scenario suppose that user is watching the iTV in the tablet and there is a TV shared.. The user can "fly out" or expand what he is watching in the TV shared. This scenario is the most interesting one. The user can extend what they are watching to other shared screen and also retrieves or "fly in" any video that is being watched in the TV.

As it has been shown three scenarios include the same options and functionalities. It is important to remark because the more complex are these functionalities the more appropriate it will be the tablet to do that. But when we do common actions that we usually do when we watch videos on Internet is when the advanced visual interfaces in a second screen can affect the user attention in a negative way (Figure 2). Also you can download a demo video in this URL: http://www.uco.es/~i02bufef/euroitv2011/demoshortvideo.ipad.mp4

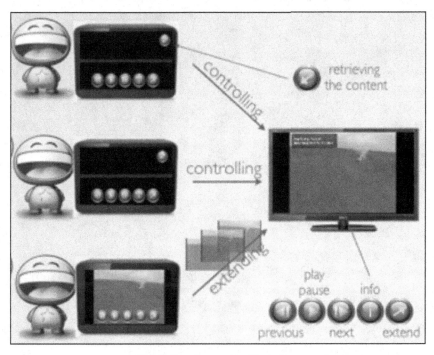

Fig. 2. Fourth scenario illustration

In summary, we are motivated by the introduction and wide adoption of small and powerful mobile computers, such as smart phones and tablets. The latter has raised the opportunity of employing them into multi-device scenarios and blending the distinction between input and output.

References

1. Cesar, P., Bulterman, D.C., Geerts, D., Jansen, J., Knoche, H., Seager, W.: Enhancing social sharing of videos: fragment, annotate, enrich, and share. In: Proceeding of the 16th ACM International Conference on Multimedia MM 2008, pp. 11–20. ACM, New York (2008)
2. Cesar, P., Bulterman, D.C.A., Jansen, J.: Leveraging the User Impact: An Architecture for Secondary Screens Usage in an Interactive Television Environment. Springer/ACM Multimedia Systems Journal (MSJ) 15(3), 127–142 (2009)
3. Fallahkhair, S., Pembertom, L., Griffiths, R.: Dual Device User Interface Design for Ubiquitous Language Learning: Mobile Phone and Interactive Television (iTV). In: IEEE International Workshop on Wireless and Mobile Technologies in Education, WMTE 2005, pp. 85–92 (2005)
4. Robertson, S., Wharton, C., Ashworth, C., Franzke, M.: Dual device user interface design: PDAs and interactive television. In: Proceedings of the SIGCHI Conference on Human Factors in Computing Systems, CHI 1996, pp. 79–86. ACM, New York (1996)

Ubiquitous Cordoba, a Cultural and Ambient Assisted Living U-City Approach

José Miguel Ramírez Uceda[1], Remedios María Robles González[1],
Enrique García Salcines[1], Francisco Javier Burón Fernández[1],
Beatriz Sainz de Abajo[2], and Carlos de Castro Lozano[1]

[1] EATCO Research Group, University of Cordoba,
Edificio Leonardo da Vinci, Campus de Rabanales, 14071, Cordoba, Spain
{p52raucj,ma1caloc,robles,egsalcines}@uco.es
[2] Telecommunications Technical School (ETSIT), University of Valladolid,
Campus Miguel Delibes, Paseo de Belén n° 15, 47011 Valladolid, Spain
beasai@tel.uva.es

Abstract. Ubiquitous Cordoba is the consequence of the development of digital communication. This has transported us into a new cultural ecosystem: the society of ubiquity. With the development of the web 2.0 and its latest versions, Internet users are granted the condition of "prosumers" (digital content producers and consumers); when they are combined with the variety of devices that result from the development of the mobile digital communication, the result is digital life. The main goal of Ubiquitous Cordoba is to empower the first accessible, usable and adaptive Ubiquitous City of the world with a special focus on elderly people, dependents, e-services and city cultural initiatives from a city with more than 3.000 years history.

Keywords: Ubiquitous city, ambient assisted living, ambient intelligence, usable, adaptive, accessible, dependent, elderly people, cultural, sustainability, energy efficiency.

1 Introduction

Ubiquitous computing is the convergence between information and communications technologies, which are present in areas as construction, appliances, health and culture among others [1].

Ubiquitous cities or U-Cities are based on ambient intelligence with a foundation of different technologies and devices such as RFID systems [2], intelligent cards, geographic location, sensorial computation and sophisticated communication networks that allow Internet connectivity for handheld devices to access remote "things" [3]. This interaction between networks, software, devices and applications enhances innovative changes to the current standards of interaction that are present in multiple aspects of day-to-day life [4].

F.V. Cipolla-Ficarra et al. (Eds.): CCGIDIS 2011, LNCS 7545, pp. 127–135, 2012.
© Springer-Verlag Berlin Heidelberg 2012

1.1   Ambient Intelligence and Ambient Assisted Living

The Ambient Intelligence paradigm makes people the focal point of future developments. Furthermore, technology has to be developed for people, instead of people adapting to technology. Ambient Intelligence applications demand integration in daily contexts in a non-intrusive way, leaving people the freedom to use the future enhanced ubiquitous systems or not.

Specifically, one of the most promising lines of development of Ambient Intelligence for human wellbeing and aging, and a key aspect we intend to integrate into our concept of the ubiquitous city is Ambient Assisted Living, which currently is focused on dependents and elderly people but whose benefits would be of interest to all inhabitants and visitors to a city [3].

Intelligent environments are responsive and sensitive to the presence of people that are integrated into a digital atmosphere that is adaptive to their needs, habits and emotions.

In general, Ambient Intelligence (AmI), are the situations in which technology becomes invisible, embedded, present whenever we need it, enabled by simple interactions, attuned to all our senses and adaptive to users and contexts.

Ambient Intelligence and Ambient Assisted Living in the context of U-Cities would solve problems like [5]:

- Recognition and adaptation for a wide variety of devices.
- Customization and adaptability of systems.
- Dynamic context intelligence.
- Support for collaboration and cooperation between distributed Ambient Intelligence components.
- Development of systems characterized by their autonomy, offering capabilities such as self-management and self-maintenance.

2   Infrastructure

Infrastructure is crucial for U-City designing [6]. In ubiquitous computing computers should not be perceived as differenced objects. Instead of this, computers should be perceived as a characteristic of things. This is known as pervasive computing, calm technology, things that think, or "everyware". In the U-City, devices are integrated around spaces where human beings could be located and where they could interact naturally with its devices and carry out any daily task transparently to his available computing capacity, usually "in the cloud."

The common point to every ubiquitous computing model is that they share the vision of being small and concealable, robust and network capable, distributed at any scale, and integratable around us without notice.

All aspects described create a very precise environment, which is not implemented in existent cities and are the real challenge of U-City implementation in existent cities.

2.1   Systems, Technologies and Devices

The main areas of knowledge infrastructure behind the ICT (information and communication technologies) that enable the construction of cities are ubiquitous sensors, communications interfaces (human-computer-human and computer-computer), and finally security information [3].

The satisfying user experience centers around the interaction between these technologies, for example, in the development of human-computer interfaces that can be used by different types of sensors / actuators. Another key point is that the system must be usable and allow a logical path toward the discovery of more complex functionality [7]. The answer to this interaction can be delivered through the available screens in multiple locations, depending on the location of the person, and these screens must be interconnected and share the user's information, which may be personal and confidential in a safe and reliable way.

Ubiquitous Computing is a major challenge, as well as a great opportunity and is an attractive area for business. Its adoption as one of the strategic development lines of the cities of a country will be reflected in a social, scientific, technological and economic impact and finally a revolution in terms of sustainability of human activities because it causes a strong paradigm shift.

Currently, knowledge and ability to be connected in cities is restricted to a level of high power consumption and low availability. While at the ubiquitous city, the immediate knowledge, activities and human relations are at a level of high availability and low power consumption. Physical movements are replaced by telecommunications with high potential for optimization across the value chain and to create new relations between the new "leisureflow" (similar to workflow but to describe the way people uses spare time).

The areas of research and development that are identified as high priority within the ubiquitous computing, and without being exhaustive, are presented below:

- Sensors.
    - Body signals acquisition.
    - RFID.
- New Generation Networks.
    - Internet 2.0 as support for ubiquitous computing..
    - Networks of sensors.
    - Ad-hoc networks.
    - Cloud computing.
    - Heterogeneous devices interconnection.
    - Security.
- Distributed systems
    - Multimedia support
    - Fault tolerance
    - Scalability
- Mobile computing
    - Peer-to-Peer
    - GIS

- GSM/GPRS positioning.
- Applications.
  - e-Health.
  - Remote health signals monitoring.
  - Context-aware systems.
  - Elderly people activity monitoring.
- Tele-Diagnosis and Tele-Assistance.

Table 1. Base technologies and integration technologies in Ubiquitous City building

Base technologies	Integration technologies
RFID	USN (Ubiquitous sensors network)
Wireless technologies	ITS (Intelligent transport systems)
Optic fiber	GIS (Geographic information systems)
Encryption (Digital signage)	LBS (Location based systems)
SoC	Home networks
	NGN/BcN (New generation networks)
	City management technologies

Most of these technologies are available today, but its use has not been widespread and many lack standardization, which makes delays in the implementation of the ubiquitous cities.

The first stage is identified by its innovation-oriented, broadband infrastructure. Fixed and mobile services continue to be traditional barriers between people and machines, with people following the instructions of the equipment. Cities with these features are referred to as B-Town (Broadband Network City).

2.2   Architecture and City Ordering for an Existent City. U-Córdoba

The biggest challenge that we find when we try to reorder and reinterpret a city for its digitalization is how to return our thinking to the very foundations of the city. The initial question is to determine what is essential in the city and what is superfluous. In our case, we find the importance of the city river and its old affluents (Figure 1), which have been converted in avenues or routes used by pedestrians. It seems to us logistically that the first space or sector in the city where Ubiquitous Córdoba should be developed is the zone of the "streams." Córdoba streams are an architectonical interpretation of the city in terms of its relationship between its original urbanism and geographic accidents.

We plan to activate a number of spaces in the "streams." Those spaces that will have a full ubiquitous implementation will be called "Shadow hot spots" (Figure 3).

We intend to carry out an activation of the spaces that will be transversally cultural and based upon the so-called "design for all" paradigm. However, other services activated will be included in the implementation (Figure 2).

Fig. 1. Cordoba, the river and old streams. Source: FAC

Design for all			
Culture and heritage			
Accomodation	Health	Education	Tourism
Transportation	Eating	Security	Administration

Fig. 2. Services in Ubiquitous Cordoba

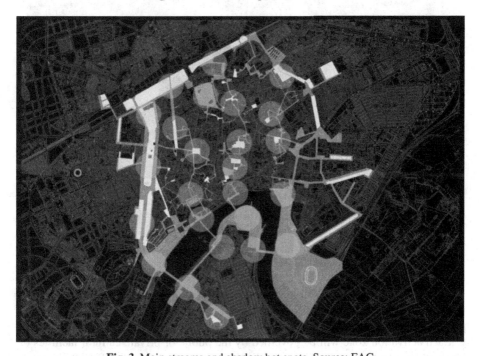

Fig. 3. Main streams and shadow hot spots. Source: FAC

People in cultural services and public buildings in the area of influence of streams and shadow hot spot are the basis for Ubiquitous Cordoba success (Figure 4). We would like to embed different layers of cultural complexity in our model as it happens in real life. People in the buildings near to the activated spaces will have the chance to participate in the city cultural program and to consume other cultural initiatives from that or from other activated space. They should be the first line "prosumers" [8] of Ubiquitous Córdoba because in the past, they have been part of the stakeholders of Cordoba's services, as consumers or as providers.

The result of all this amalgam will be AAL services enabled to plan spare time integrated with the planning needs.

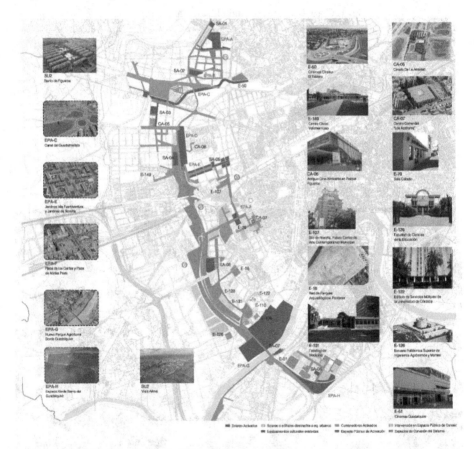

Fig. 4. Equipment and buildings at Cultural Stream number 1. Source: FAC

In addition, these spaces will include technological elements of activation based in non-conventional interactive displays as interactive wall systems, digital graffiti, 3D projection, virtual worlds or avatars.

Each activation zone will be governed by the public or private cultural facilities of importance attached to it. These facilities act as synapses of different "cultural neurons" that are distributed in various shadow hot spots. Likewise, businesses, private spaces or homes could collaborate around the cultural spaces created.

Information will be generated on several levels, but the user receives a consistent, coherent response according to their personal tastes. The information will be tracked through various multi-agent collaborative systems of intelligent adaptive hypermedia and will come from the following sources:

- The city
- The cultural activator of that zone
- The cultural activator of building around the zone
- Other activated zones.
- The users of the "friends" group
- Any user of the system

So all the spaces are enabled by the interactivity through the cultural streams and especially in shadow hot spots, and every user is a prosumer. Because of the ubiquitous display systems for interactive digital content, these will differ depending on the devices available for interaction:

- Browser: collaborative tourist content and virtual museums.
- Tablet: virtual 360° recreation of the city with enhanced multimedia content.
- LED outdoor screen: stereoscopic video streaming broadcast of cultural event with social networks integration.

3   User Experience

Satisfactory experience for the user will be achieved through focusing on the interaction between multiple technologies. An example of this would be computer-human interfaces, which can be used with a wide variety of devices. A key emphasis should be on usability, which enables the user to discover advanced functionalities that are hidden at first sight. The answer to U-City user intuitive and automated interaction could be delivered through "screens" distributed in multiple areas, depending on the geographic position of the person.

The concept of *distributed screens* does not indicate the deployment of a static network of screens as in a digital signage concept. Following our view, a "screen" is a PC, a laptop, a tablet, a smart-phone, an information kiosk, an interactive shop window system, a 3D projection or a digital entertainment device that recognizes audience and personalizes the experience based on a mix of personal profiles of the people attending the current information channel. Accessible and usable systems for dependants and elderly people will be fully capable of retrieving any information in the ubiquitous city. An example of this kind of device is the iFreeTablet and Siesta Operative System. [9], [10].

In U-Córdoba, digital devices will be information receiver systems that change into remote controllers when they are combined with other systems such as digital entertainment devices, 3D projections or LED screens which allow for a high level of collaborative socio cultural interaction with the elements of the U-City dwelling complex social contexts [11]. They also will provide a new level of distributed creativity, making cities heterogeneous "living" entities [12] that add value to the citizens and to all the companies involved in the value chain around the U-City and its associated services [13].

4   Future Developments

At an initial stage, a series of U-Córdoba public spaces will be active with a limited number of e-services. These spaces will be of touristic, cultural and economic importance to the city. Stage two of the project will be to join these spaces through corridors called "cultural streams". Corridors have been designed for pedestrian use. Stage three will be to create new ubiquitous spaces in public facilities at adjacent neighborhoods and in the river Guadalquivir. Stage four will be to expand the U-Córdoba spaces to all Spanish high-speed train stations. Stage five will be to finally expand U-Córdoba to the entire city and the availability of a broad number of e-services.

5   Conclusions

U-Córdoba has a unique opportunity to exploit the Internet content on their behalf, not only studying and possibly adopting best practices from other cities in the world, but also projecting their information online for local and international use. Internet, a potential generator of different forms of economic prosperity, allows the attractive aspects of a city (infrastructure, culture, geography, tourism) to be disseminated almost instantaneously, providing access to a global audience like never before. In this sense, only a dynamic generation of local content involving various stakeholders in the city will allow cities to be exposed to the world as an attractive destination for investment, tourism, culture, and leisure. Other indirect benefits such as sustainability and human development will come alone as part of the new ecosystem created.

References

1. Cho, H.S., Cho, B.S., Park, W.H.: Ubiquitous-City Bussiness Strategies: The case of South Korea. In: PICMET, pp. 1147–1153 (2007)
2. Kim, H.S., Sohn, S.Y.: Cost of ownership model for the RFID logistics system applcable to u-city. European Journal of Operational Research 194, 406–417 (2009)
3. Park, W.H., Jeong, W.S., Cho, H.: A Study of the Evolution of the U-City Service. PICMET, 1141–1146 (2007)
4. Komninos, N.: The Architecture of Intelligent Cities: Integraing Human, Collective and Intelligence to Enhance Knowledge and Innovation. In: 2nd IET International Conference, pp. 13–20 (2006)
5. Lee, M., et al.: An Urban Computing Framework for Autonomous Services in a U-City. In: Convergence Information Technology, Gyeongju, pp. 645–650 (2007)

6. Choi, J.H.-J.: The city is connections:Seoul as an urban network. In: Multimedia Systems, vol. 16, pp. 75–84. Springer (2010)

7. de Castro Lozano, C., Salcines, E.G., Sainz de Abajo, B., Burón Fernández, F.J., Ramírez, J.M., Recellado, J.G.Z., Montoya, R.S., Bell, J., Marin, F.A.: Usable Interface Design for Everyone. In: Cipolla Ficarra, F.V., de Castro Lozano, C., Nicol, E., Kratky, A., Cipolla-Ficarra, M. (eds.) HCITOCH 2010. LNCS, vol. 6529, pp. 157–172. Springer, Heidelberg (2011)

8. Islas, O.: La sociedad de la Ubicuidad, los prosumidores y un modelo de comunicación para comprender la complejidad de las comunicaciones digitales. In: ALAIC (Asociación Latinoamericana de Investigación de la Comunicación), vol. 7, pp. 68–77 (2007)

9. de Castro, C., García, E., Rámirez, J.M., Burón, F.J., Sainz, B., Sánchez, R., Robles, R.M., Torres, J.C., Bell, J., Alcantud, F.: SIeSTA: Aid Technology and e-Service Integrated System. In: Cipolla Ficarra, F.V., de Castro Lozano, C., Pérez Jiménez, M., Nicol, E., Kratky, A., Cipolla-Ficarra, M. (eds.) ADNTIIC 2010. LNCS, vol. 6616, pp. 159–170. Springer, Heidelberg (2011)

10. de Castro Lozano, C., Salcines, E.G., Sainz de Abajo, B., Burón Fernández, F.J., Ramírez, J.M., Recellado, J.G.Z., Montoya, R.S., Bell, J., Marin, F.A.: SIeSTA: From Concept Board to Concept Desktop. In: Cipolla Ficarra, F.V., de Castro Lozano, C., Nicol, E., Kratky, A., Cipolla-Ficarra, M. (eds.) HCITOCH 2010. LNCS, vol. 6529, pp. 173–183. Springer, Heidelberg (2011)

11. Shklovski, I., Chang, M.: Urban Computing: Navigating Space and Context. Computer 39(9), 36–37

12. Williams, A., Dourish, P.: Imagining the City: the cultural dimensions of Urban Computing. Computer, 38–43 (2006)

13. Jeong, W.S., Cho, B.S., Kim, P.R.: An Analysis of the Economic Effects for Launching the Ubiquitous City. PICMET, 1154–1159 (2007)

Modeling Parallel Applications on Mobile Devices

Daniel Giulianelli[1], Claudia Pons[2], Carina González[3], Pablo Vera[1],
Rocío Rodríguez[1], and Víctor Fernández[1]

[1] National University of La Matanza
Department of Engineering and Technological Researches
Florencio Varela 1903, San Justo, Buenos Aires, Argentina
[2] School of Computer Science
Street 50 and 150 La Plata, Buenos Aires, Argentina
[3] La Laguna University
Technical High School of Computer Engineering
Pabellón de Gobierno, c/ Molinos de Agua s/n – 38200 La Laguna, Spain
dgiulian@unlam.edu.ar, cpons@lifia.info.unlp.edu.ar,
cjgonza@ull.es, pablovera@unlam.edu.ar,
{rrodri,vfernandez}@unlam.edu.ar

Abstract. Nowadays more and more users have mobile devices with high computing power. This fact allows taking advantage of that processing power to design applications that allow users to interact remotely with the system simply using, for example, their cell phones. This requires having a modeling tool that allows incorporating the concepts of mobile computing and their particular domain characteristics. This work shows an extension to the UML profile called PROCODI (Concurrent and Distributed Processes), which adds the possibility of incorporating mobile devices as nodes within the model. This fact allows a quick visualization using a single diagram, of structural and behavioral aspects of the system, also including, now, mobile devices with their peculiarities.

Keywords: Mobile Computing, UML, Profile, Distributed Computing.

1 Introduction

The use of mobile devices in the field of Enterprise applications began several years ago. Initially it began by taking advantage of the capabilities of PDA (Personal Data Assistant) type devices like Palm, Symbian or Pocket PC. These devices had limited processing power, limited memory and their connectivity capabilities were not permanent. A little bit later other devices emerged that were able to combine the connectivity features of cell phones with multipurpose operating systems like, for example, windows mobile, creating the firsts smart phones. With these devices, despite of still lacking of computing power and memory, the users had a permanent connection, because of the capability of connecting to the cell phone network, opening the possibilities of making connected interactive applications, where the user

F.V. Cipolla-Ficarra et al. (Eds.): CCGIDIS 2011, LNCS 7545, pp. 136–143, 2012.

is capable of interacting with the system without a fixed location. However these devices where not massively used, and they were limited to some particular sectors.

Nowadays mobile technology has progressed considerably and continues with a fast growth every day. There are in the market a great diversity of cell phones with a processing power that far exceeds the power of Palm or Pocket PC devices, and that is close to a desktop computer. These new mobile devices are not limited to cell phone because Tablet PC devices are becoming popular with devices like Apple IPAD, Motorolla Xoom, Blackberry Playbook, etc becoming a continuous growing's field. Most of these devices, cell phones and tables, have several ways of internet connectivity, like WIFI, GPRS, EDGE and 3G. The hardware's advance makes that, when designing applications, designers start thinking that it might be running on both a desktop and a mobile device, where, although it will require some adaptation for example for displaying on small screens, its processing capabilities allow considering more complex applications.

One of the main subjects that must be considered when designing an application is to take advantage of the multiprocessing capabilities of the new mobile operating systems, where, with or without the presence of multiple cores, it is possible to run several threads simultaneously, speeding heavy processing tasks in the applications. Therefore, when modeling a distributed and/ or parallel application, it should be considered that the application could also be used in a mobile device because it could be seen as one more processing node in a particular application with similar features of a fixed node.

2   Extension of UML Profile PROCODI

In 2010 the research team finished the design and building of a profile based on UML [2] which main goal was to model parallel and concurrent applications in an easy way by using a single diagram that allows identifying:

- The different nodes involved in the application
- The communication channels between the nodes
- Activities that run simultaneously by the specification of the tasks of each thread
- Generic parallelizable activities which are distributed automatically on different threads.
- Access to shared resources and signaling

This work shows and extension to PROCODI to allow modeling parallel and distributed applications that include mobile devices as some of the nodes. For that purpose the following characteristics have been added to the profile:

- Mobile device: represents the nodes that can change their location.

These devices are:

- o   cell phones,
- o   tablets,
- o   PDAs,
- o   etc.

- Location: the fixed place where a mobile device can interact with the system. For example a Bluetooth connection in the station A of the subway.
- Mobile Location: if the mobile device is being moved within a transport with connectivity. For example a plane or a train with WIFI connection.
- Text messages: represents the SMS messages to and from the mobile device.
- Bluetooth messages: represents messages from and to the mobile device that are made with a Bluetooth connection so the distance between the sender and the receiver is limited.
- GPS: Represents the use of the location capabilities of the mobile device using the satellite positioning system.

By including these characteristic to the existing profile, the particularities of the mobile devices will be shown in the model allowing:

1. Differentiating the mobile devices of the system and their location allowing switching between fixed and mobiles scenarios.
2. Modeling the necessary actions that must be performed when the mobile device is moving from one scenario to other.
3. Modeling cell phones' own characteristics like, for example, SMS text messages, or the use of the GPS.

Figure 1 shows the full class diagram of PROCODI profile with the extensions for mobile devices (in green).

Table 1 shows the association among the elements of the extension and the UML metaclasses in which the stereotypes are defined.

The stereotypes generate new metaclasses that can be also extended.

Table 1. Association between elements of the extension and UML metaclasses

Profile Element	Stereotypes	UML Metaclass
Mobile Device	ProMobileDevice	Node
Location	ProLocation	Class
Mobile Location	ProMobileLocation	ProLocation
Text Message	ProSMSMessage	ProExtendedMessage
BlueTooth Message	ProBluetoothMessage	ProExtendedMessage
GPS Location	ProGPSLocation	Class

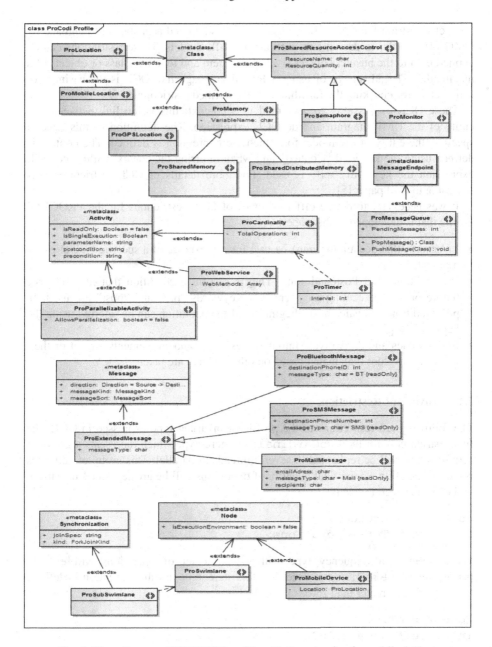

Fig. 1. Class diagram of PROCODI profile with the extension for mobile devices

3   Restrictions

Restrictions are defined for PROCODI and for the domain of mobile devices. Although restrictions could have been created using natural language, OCL [8]

(Object Constrain Language) was choose. OCL is adopted as a standard language by OMG [4] in order to describe restrictions in UML models. These restrictions can be applied both to the business object level of a system and to a metaclass or objects of a metamodel. The advantage of using a formal language like OCL is the easiness of using a tool for checking the fulfillment of the defined restrictions.

These OCL expressions are executed in a context; this is the link between one entity of the UML diagram and de OCL expression. The definition of this context specifies the entity of the model for which the expression is defined. The context is defined using the keyword "Context" and when referring the context within the OCL expression the keyword "self" is used. For more details of OCL restrictions it is advisable to read paper [5].

It was necessary to define different types of OCL restrictions for the PROCODI profile that is developed in this paper:

- Invariants: this declaration must be true for all instance of a specific type at every moment.
- Preconditions and Postconditions: They represent a condition that must be true before or after executing an operation. Keywords "pre" and "post" are used. In postconditions the value at the beginning of the operation can be referred using the keyword "@pre"
- Initial values and derivatives: Initial values of the model elements are set or their derivatives values (calculated based on other values) are taken

3.1 Invariant Restrictions

The following are restrictions of the profile of invariant type expressed in OCL The first restriction is for the ProCardinality stereotype which represents a group of activities that will be replicated in several threads in parallel. This group of activities is called operation, so the final quantity of operations will be greater than 1 because it will execute several threads.

```
Contex ProCardinality
inv : self.TotalOperations>1
```

When defining a frequency type with which a set of operations will execute periodically the ProTimer is used. For this stereotype, a time restriction is defined to set the range greater than zero.

```
Contex ProTimer
inv : self.Interval>0
```

Every defined Webservice must have at least one method. The OCL expression to represent this is:

```
Contex ProWebService
inv : self.WebMethods -> size()>0
```

Monitors and semaphores must have a quantity of resource to control at least of 1

```
Contex ProSharedResourceAccessControl
inv : self.ResourceQuantity >0
```

In the three classes that derive from ProExtendedMessage the message type must be declared. The message could not be change in any class instance.

```
Contex ProMailMessage
inv : messageType="Mail"
Contex ProSMSMessage
inv : messageType="SMS"
Contex ProBluetoothMessage
inv : messageType="BT"
```

3.2   Pre/Post Condition Restrictions

For the message's queue the OCL restrictions express that, when the message counter is greater than zero and then a pending message is took in order to be process, the message counter value will be decrease in one, which is the message that has been dequeue.

```
Contex ProMessageQueue::PopMessage():Class
pre: self.PendingMessages>0
post: self.PendingMessages=self.PendingMessages@pre -1
```

A similar restriction is used to queue messages

```
Contex ProMessageQueue::PushMessage(message:Class):Void
pre: messages->notEmpty()
post:self.PendingMessages=self.PendingMessages@pre+1
```

3.3   Initial Values and Derivatives Restrictions

It was necessary to write a restriction to set the initial default value for the attribute "AllowsParallelization" of the class ProActivity. So, by default, no activity is parallelizable unless stated.

```
Contex ProActivity::AllowsParallelization::Boolean
init:  -> false
```

4   Related Work

There are several works related with representing mobility in UML. Some of them are:

- "UML Profile to Model Mobile Systems" [3]: This work shows the characteristic adaptations in the design of applications that operate in the mobile computing area. It defines artifacts to identify several aspects of mobile applications like for example: Place, NodeLocation, MobileElement, MobileCode, CurrentDeployment, AllowDeployment, MobilityManager, MoveActivities. It also includes the mobile code paradigm that allows modifying the load of the objects and the traffic between them to adapt to the current node condition and the network load.
- Another interesting work is from the University of München in Germany [6]. It shows an extension of the class and activity diagrams of UML to model mobile systems. The extensions that apply are based in the use of stereotypes and are useful for identifying mobile objects, locations and activities like, for example, mobility or cloning.
- In the work of Flabio Oquendo [1] the architecture description language (ADL) is applied to design mobile agents. ADL is presented as a UML profile that includes a graphical representation using implementation diagrams and components.
- The work shown in [7] extends UML for allowing the real time representation, tracking and management of mobile objects.

5   Conclusions

Modeling a parallel and distributed system requires the use of several UML diagrams for representing each one of its characteristics. With the extensions made to PROCODI it´s possible by means of a single extended activity diagram, to visualize both structural and behavioral aspects simultaneously.

This is especially profitable when modeling distributed applications because it allows seeing the nodes and their interconnection, faster.

By extending this model adding the mobile devices, all benefits of PROCODI are taken and it is powered by making seamless the modeling of mobile applications by treating the mobile devices as another node of the model, but including their particular communication characteristics. It also allows modeling different scenarios taking in consideration the geographical position of the device.

As future work we propose to model server applications with this extension of PROCODI.

References

1. Oquendo, F.: An Architecture Description Language based on the Higher-Order Typed π-Calculus for Specifying Dynamic and Mobile Software Architectures. University of Savoie at Annecy ESIA – LISTIC Lab – Formal Software Architecture and Process Research Group, France (2004), http://portal.acm.org/citation.cfm?id=986728
2. Giulianelli, D.A., Pons, C., Rodríguez, R.A., Vera, P.M., Fernandez, V.M.: A Profile´s Design for Parallel Applications Modelling. Revista Colombiana de Computación (Colombian Journal of Computing) 11(1), 56–68 (2010), ISBN: 1657-2831; Universidad Autónoma de Bucaramanga. Editores: Alina Fedossova, Eduardo Carrillo Zambrano. Formato: 137 páginas

3. Grassi, V., Mirandola, R., Sabetta, A.: A UML Profile to Model Mobile Systems. Universit'a di Roma "Tor Vergata", Italy (2004)
4. OMG (Object Management Group). "Catalog of UML Profile of Specification" (2009), http://www.omg.org/technology/documents/profile_catalog.html
5. Becker, V., Pons, C.: Definición Formal de la Semántica de UML-OCL a través de su traducción a OBJECT-Z, Universidad Nacional de La Plata, Facultad de Informática, pp. 2–6 (2003)
6. Baumeister, H., Koch, N., Kosiuczenko, P., Wirsing, M.: Extending Activity Diagrams to Model Mobile Systems. Institut fur Informatik Ludwig-Maximilians-Universiat Munchen, Germany (2003),
   http://www.springerlink.com/content/fec97clg6c2aw6qj/
7. El Bouziri, A., Boulmakoul, A., Mouncif, H., Mohamed: Modeling Mobile Object for Transportation Information System and Mobile GIS., LIST Lab., Computer Sciences Department Mohammedia Faculty of Sciences and Technology (FSTM), Moroco (2005)
8. OMG. Object Constraint Language (2011),
   http://www.omg.org/spec/OCL/2.3/Beta2

Author Index

Acuña, Silvia T. 94
Alma, Jacqueline 28

Burón Fernández, Francisco Javier 112, 122, 127

Castro, John W. 94
Chu, Chi-Fang 67
Cipolla Ficarra, Francisco V. 1, 28, 51, 79
Cipolla-Ficarra, Miguel 28

de Castro Lozano, Carlos 112, 122, 127

Fernández, Víctor 136
Ficarra, Valeria M. 79

García Salcines, Enrique 112, 122, 127
Giulianelli, Daniel 136
González, Carina 136
González, Remedios María Robles 127
González-González, Carina S. 104

Huang, Chih-Fang 14, 67

Kammueller, Florian 42
Ko, Shu-Fang 14
Kratky, Andreas 79

López Coronado, Miguel 112

Mena, Rafael 122

Pons, Claudia 136

Rodríguez, Rocío 136

Sainz de Abajo, Beatriz 112, 122, 127
Sánchez González, Javier 112
Socas-Guerra, Victor 104

Uceda, José Miguel Ramírez 127

Vera, Pablo 136